HAMLYN
NEW
ALL COLOUR
COOKBOOK

HAMLYN
NEW
ALL COLOUR
COOKBOOK

Front cover shows, left to right: *Iced cucumber soup (recipe 1), Beef in beer (recipe 61), Citrus queen of puddings (recipe 193).*

Half title page shows, left to right: *Vegetable pancakes (recipe 129), Carrot cake (recipe 261).*

Title page shows, left to right: *Roast chicken (recipe 81), Rich tuna mousse (recipe 25), Wholemeal bread (recipe 241).*

Back cover shows, clockwise from top to left: *Fish kebabs (recipe 41), Chicken liver risotto (recipe 145), Baked potatoes (recipe 105), Chilled strawberry creams (recipe 217), Coffee and hazelnut gâteau (recipe 285), Sausage layer pie (recipe 169).*

First published in Great Britain in 1986
by Hamlyn, an imprint of Reed Consumer Books Limited
Michelin House, 81 Fulham Road, London SW3 6RB
and Auckland, Melbourne, Singapore and Toronto

12th impression 1993

Photography by David Jordan and Timothy Rose
Styling by Pip Kelly
Line drawings by Roberta Colegate-Stone and Gay John
Galsworthy

A CIP catalogue record for this book is available from the
British Library

ISBN 0 600 57527 6

Produced by Mandarin Offset
Printed and bound in China

OTHER TITLES IN THIS SERIES INCLUDE
Hamlyn All Colour Salads
Hamlyn All Colour Entertaining
Hamlyn All Colour Vegetarian Cookbook
Hamlyn All Colour Chinese Cookbook
Hamlyn All Colour Indian Cookbook

CONTENTS

SOUPS   1 - 24

STARTERS & SNACKS   25 - 40

FISH DISHES   41 - 60

CASSEROLES & STEWS   61 - 80

ROASTS & GRILLS   81 - 104

VEGETABLES & SALADS   105 - 128

VEGETARIAN RECIPES   129 - 144

RICE & PASTA   145 - 168

PIES, FLANS & PASTIES   169 - 192

HOT PUDDINGS   193 - 216

COOL DESSERTS   217 - 240

BREADS & SCONES   241 - 260

FAMILY CAKES & BISCUITS   261 - 284

FANCY CAKES   285 - 304

Useful facts and figures

NOTES ON METRICATION

In this book quantities are given in metric and Imperial measures. Exact conversion from Imperial to metric measures does not usually give very convenient working quantities and so the metric measures have been rounded off into units of 25 grams. The table below shows the recommended equivalents.

Ounces	Approx g to nearest whole figure	Recommended conversion to nearest unit of 25	Ounces	Approx g to nearest whole figure	Recommended conversion to nearest unit of 25
1	28	25	9	255	250
2	57	50	10	283	275
3	85	75	11	312	300
4	113	100	12	340	350
5	142	150	13	368	375
6	170	175	14	396	400
7	198	200	15	425	425
8	227	225	16(1lb)	454	450

Note

When converting quantities over 16 oz first add the appropriate figures in the centre column, then adjust to the nearest unit of 25. As a general guide, 1 kg (1000 g) equals 2.2 lb or about 2 lb 3 oz. This method of conversion gives good results in nearly all cases, although in certain pastry and cake recipes a more accurate conversion is necessary to produce a balanced recipe.

Liquid measures

The millilitre has been used in this book and the following table gives a few examples.

Imperial	Approx ml to nearest whole figure	Recommended ml	Imperial	Approx ml to nearest whole figure	Recommended ml
¼ pint	142	150 ml	1 pint	567	600 ml
½ pint	283	300 ml	1½ pints	851	900 ml
¾ pint	425	450 ml	1¾ pints	992	1000 ml (1 litre)

Spoon measures

All spoon measures given in this book are level unless otherwise stated.

Can sizes

At present, cans are marked with the exact (usually to the nearest whole number) metric equivalent of the Imperial weight of the contents, so we have followed this practice when giving can sizes.

Oven temperatures

The table below gives recommended equivalents.

	°C	°F	Gas Mark		°C	°F	Gas Mark
Very cool	110	225	¼	Moderately hot	190	375	5
	120	250	½		200	400	6
Cool	140	275	1	Hot	220	425	7
	150	300	2		230	450	8
Moderate	160	325	3	Very hot	240	475	9
	180	350	4				

NOTES FOR AMERICAN AND AUSTRALIAN USERS

In America the 8 fl oz measuring cup is used. In Australia metric measures are now used in conjunction with the standard 250 ml measuring cup. The Imperial pint, used in Britain and Australia, is 20 fl oz, while the American pint is 16 fl oz. It is important to remember that the Australian tablespoon differs from both the British and American tablespoons; the table below gives a comparison. The British standard tablespoon, which has been used throughout this book, holds 17.7 ml, the American 14.2 ml, and the Australian 20 ml. A teaspoon holds approximately 5 ml in all three countries.

British	American	Australian
1 teaspoon	1 teaspoon	1 teaspoon
1 tablespoon	1 tablespoon	1 tablespoon
2 tablespoons	3 tablespoons	2 tablespoons
3½ tablespoons	4 tablespoons	3 tablespoons
4 tablespoons	5 tablespoons	3½ tablespoons

AN IMPERIAL/AMERICAN GUIDE TO SOLID AND LIQUID MEASURES

Imperial	American	Imperial	American
Solid measures		**Liquid measures**	
1 lb butter or margarine	2 cups	¼ pint liquid	⅔ cup liquid
1 lb flour	4 cups	½ pint	1¼ cups
1 lb granulated or caster sugar	2 cups	¾ pint	2 cups
1 lb icing sugar	3 cups	1 pint	2½ cups
8 oz rice	1 cup	1½ pints	3¾ cups
		2 pints	5 cups (2½ pints)

NOTE: WHEN MAKING ANY OF THE RECIPES IN THIS BOOK, ONLY FOLLOW ONE SET OF MEASURES AS THEY ARE NOT INTERCHANGEABLE.

INTRODUCTION

The Hamlyn New All Colour Cookbook is a must for those starting to cook basic dishes as well as for experienced cooks who wish to enlarge their repertoire of dishes for family meals, dinner parties and other special occasions.

Every recipe is illustrated by a colour photograph so that you can see just what the finished dish should look like as you are following the recipe. Attractive presentation of food greatly increases the pleasure of a meal, so the opportunity to check on the garnish and appearance of the dish provided by the photograph is invaluable. Not only does every one of this huge collection of recipes give excellent results, each is easy to follow and accompanied by a microwave, freezer, or cook's tip, describing a technique for use in all kinds of basic food preparation and cookery. Detailed drawings beside the tips give further clarification. And for weight- and health-conscious cooks, the calorie count of each recipe is provided.

When you want to plan an ideal meal or dinner party, this book will give you numerous appetising ideas. Just leaf through from soups and starters at the beginning of the book, to fish, main dishes, vegetables and cool and hot desserts, and be tempted to try something new. There is a section of vegetarian meals for those who want to limit the amount of meat in their diet and another on rice and pasta dishes. Nor is home baking forgotten; there are chapters on pies, pasties and flans, breads and scones, family cakes and biscuits and fancy cakes for those seasonal special occasion teas.

There is no need to worry about how long preparation of a meal will take, because a further indispensable feature of the Hamlyn New All Colour Cookbook is that preparation and cooking times are given for each recipe, so that you can see at a glance whether you have time to make a particular dish.

All the recipes have been tested and we are sure you will agree that they not only look and taste delicious, but that they are easy and quick to prepare.

Note When this book was first published cling film was used in the microwave oven. Since then, it has been recommended that *ordinary cling film should not be used for microwave cooking*. Substitute **special microwave cling film**, a plate, or a suitable lid to cover food.

SOUPS

Home-made soups are delicious and very versatile. A chilled or light cream soup makes a simple, cook-ahead starter for a dinner party. More substantial soups such as minestrone or French onion make a tasty light lunch, when served with hot herb bread. Chunky chowders or soups with pasta or dumplings are welcome weekend supper dishes on cold evenings.

1   ICED CUCUMBER SOUP

Preparation time:
5 minutes, plus 1 hour to chill

Cooking time:
25 minutes

Serves 6

Calories:
85 per portion

YOU WILL NEED:
1 large cucumber
1 onion
900 ml/1½ pints chicken stock
25 g/1 oz butter or margarine
25 g/1 oz plain flour
salt and pepper
150 ml/¼ pint natural yogurt
FOR THE GARNISH
18 ice cubes
mint sprigs
cucumber slices

Dice the cucumber, and finely chop the onion. Place the cucumber in a saucepan with the stock and onion. Bring to the boil, cover and simmer for about 20 minutes, or until the cucumber is tender. Cool, then blend in a liquidizer until smooth.

Melt the butter or margarine in a saucepan, stir in the flour and cook for 1 minute. Gradually add the cucumber purée. Bring to the boil, stirring frequently, then reduce the heat and simmer for 2 minutes. Season to taste. Add the natural yogurt and leave to cool thoroughly.

Garnish each serving with ice cubes, mint sprigs and cucumber slices.

2   SPANISH SOUP

Preparation time:
10 minutes, plus 2 hours to chill

Serves 6

Calories:
90 per portion

YOU WILL NEED:
½ cucumber
450 g/1 lb tomatoes
1 red pepper
1 green pepper
2 large Spanish onions
1 garlic clove
100 g/4 oz fresh white breadcrumbs
about 450 ml/¾ pint water
2 tablespoons red wine vinegar
1 teaspoon salt
2 teaspoons olive oil
½ teaspoon paprika
chopped parsley, to garnish

Chop the cucumber, peel and chop the tomatoes, seed and chop the peppers. Chop the onions and garlic.

In a bowl mix the vegetables with the garlic, breadcrumbs, water, vinegar and salt. Blend the mixture in a liquidizer until smooth, then return it to the bowl and whisk in the oil and paprika.

Cover the soup and put it in the refrigerator for 2 hours.

Before serving the soup, stir well, then ladle into chilled soup bowls. Garnish each serving with parsley.

■ COOK'S TIP

Before adding the yogurt, whisk a tablespoon of mint jelly into the hot soup until dissolved.

■ COOK'S TIP

To peel tomatoes, put them in a basin, cover with boiling water, leave for 30 seconds, then strip off skins.

3 VICHYSOISSE

Preparation time:
25 minutes, plus 1
hour to chill

Cooking time:
20 minutes

Serves 6

Calories:
260 per portion

YOU WILL NEED:
2 large leeks
1 onion
1 large potato
50 g/2 oz butter or margarine
600 ml/1 pint hot vegetable stock
300 ml/½ pint milk
150 ml/¼ pint double or whipping
  cream
150 ml/¼ pint natural yogurt
salt and pepper
dash of Tabasco sauce
2 tablespoons chopped chives

Wash and trim the leeks, then cut into thin rings. Finely chop the onion. Peel and dice the potato.

In a saucepan cook the onion and leeks in the butter or margarine until softened. Add the potato and stock. Bring to the boil, reduce the heat and simmer gently for 20 minutes. Add the milk. Blend the soup in a liquidizer until smooth. Transfer to a bowl and whisk in the cream, yogurt, salt and pepper and Tabasco.

Leave the vichysoisse to cool. When cold, chill for at least 1 hour.

Serve the soup in individual bowls and garnish each serving with freshly chopped chives.

4 CHILLED LEMON SOUP

Preparation time:
5-10 minutes, plus 1
hour to chill

Cooking time:
25 minutes

Serves 6

Calories:
195 per portion

YOU WILL NEED:
1 onion
1 garlic clove
50 g/2 oz butter or margarine
25 g/1 oz plain flour
900 ml/1½ pints chicken stock
grated rind and juice of 2 lemons
salt and pepper
300 ml/½ pint single cream
FOR THE GARNISH
thin lemon slices
freshly chopped mint

Finely chop the onion and garlic. In a saucepan, cook the onion and garlic in the butter or margarine until softened. Reduce the heat, stir in the flour, then gradually add the stock, stirring continuously, and bring to the boil. Add the lemon rind, juice and seasoning to taste. Reduce the heat and simmer gently for 20 minutes.

Blend the soup in a liquidizer, then pour it into a large tureen and stir in the cream. Cool and chill for at least 1 hour.

Just before serving garnish with slices of lemon and freshly chopped mint.

■ COOK'S TIP

To clean leeks, trim off roots and tough green leaves. Slit leeks lengthways to centre, then hold root end uppermost under cold tap to wash out dirt.

■ FREEZER TIP

Boil home-made stocks rapidly until greatly reduced. Cool, freeze in ice cube trays then pack cubes in freezer bags. Dilute with water before use.

5 HOT AVOCADO SOUP

Preparation time:
20 minutes

Cooking time:
20 minutes

Serves 6

Calories:
300 per portion

YOU WILL NEED:
3 ripe avocados
2 tablespoons lemon juice
1 onion, finely chopped
2 garlic cloves, finely chopped
1 green chilli, seeded and thinly sliced
50 g/2 oz butter or margarine
25 g/1 oz plain flour
900 ml/1½ pints chicken stock
150 ml/¼ pint milk
salt and pepper
150 ml/¼ pint soured cream

Quarter the avocados. Remove the stones and peel and discard. Cut off a few thin slices of avocado and reserve them for garnish. Brush with a little of the lemon juice to prevent discoloration. Roughly chop the remaining avocado and mix it with the remaining lemon juice.

Cook the onion, garlic and chilli in the butter or margarine until softened. Reduce the heat, add the flour, cook for 2 minutes, stirring. Add the chicken stock and milk, stirring all the time. Bring to the boil, add the avocado and seasoning, then reduce the heat and simmer gently for 2-3 minutes. Blend in a liquidizer until smooth. Return the soup to the saucepan and over a very low heat stir in the soured cream.

Pour the soup into individual soup bowls and garnish each serving with the reserved slices of avocado. Serve immediately.

6 CARROT SOUP

Preparation time:
10 minutes

Cooking time:
25 minutes

Serves 6

Calories:
200 per portion

YOU WILL NEED:
675 g/1½ lb carrots, sliced
salt and pepper
1 onion
2 celery sticks
25 g/1 oz butter or margarine
25 g/1 oz plain flour
900 ml/1½ pints chicken stock
1 × 400 g/14 oz can evaporated milk
2 teaspoons lemon juice
FOR THE GARNISH
grated carrots
2 tablespoons chopped parsley

Cook the carrots in boiling salted water for 15 minutes, then drain them.

Chop the onion and celery and fry in the butter or margarine until softened, but not browned. Reduce the heat and stir in the flour. Add the carrots. Slowly add the stock and evaporated milk, stirring continuously. Add the lemon juice. Bring to the boil, reduce the heat and simmer gently for 5 minutes. Season to taste. Blend the soup in a liquidizer, then return it to a saucepan and reheat.

Pour the soup into individual soup bowls and garnish with grated carrot and freshly chopped parsley.

■ COOK'S TIP

To ripen avocados quickly, place in a brown paper bag with a ripe banana or tomato.

■ MICROWAVE TIP

Put vegetables in a bowl and add 300 ml/½ pint boiling stock. Cover, leaving a gap for steam to escape, and cook on full power for 18-20 minutes. Liquidize. Mix the *flour to a paste with cold water, stir in the remaining boiling stock and add to the soup. Stir in evaporated milk, seasoning and juice. Heat for 5-7 minutes.*

7 TOMATO AND ORANGE SOUP

Preparation time: 10 minutes	**YOU WILL NEED:**
	1 onion, chopped
	2 garlic cloves, crushed
Cooking time: 20 minutes	*50 g/2 oz butter or margarine*
	25 g/1 oz plain flour
Serves 6	*1 × 800g/28oz can chopped tomatoes*
	900 ml/1½ pints chicken stock
Calories: 130 per portion	*grated rind and juice of 2 oranges*
	2 teaspoons sugar
	salt and pepper
	FOR THE GARNISH
	150 ml/¼ pint single cream
	grated rind of 1 orange

Fry the onion and garlic in the butter or margarine until softened. Stir in the flour, then the tomatoes. Stirring continuously, add the stock and the orange rind and juice. Reduce the heat and simmer gently for 15 minutes, stirring occasionally. Add the sugar and season to taste. For a smooth soup, blend in a liquidizer.

Pour the soup into individual bowls and garnish each serving with a swirl of cream and a sprinkle of orange rind.

8 CREAM OF WATERCRESS SOUP

Preparation time: 10 minutes	**YOU WILL NEED:**
	1 onion, chopped
	2 garlic cloves, crushed
Cooking time: 10 minutes	*50 g/2 oz butter or margarine*
	50 g/2 oz plain flour
Serves 6	*600 ml/1 pint chicken stock*
	600 ml/1 pint milk
Calories: 225 per portion	*2 bunches of watercress, trimmed and chopped*
	salt and pepper
	¼ teaspoon grated nutmeg
	juice of ½ lemon
	150 ml/¼ pint single cream
	watercress sprigs, to garnish

In a saucepan, fry the onion and garlic in the butter or margarine until softened. Reduce the heat and stir in the flour. Gradually add the stock and milk, stirring all the time. Stir in the watercress, salt and pepper, nutmeg and lemon juice. Simmer gently for 5 minutes. Reduce the heat, then stir in the single cream. Reheat without boiling.

Pour the soup into individual soup bowls and garnish each serving with a sprig of watercress.

■ FREEZER TIP

Pour cooled soup into a rigid plastic container, leaving head space for expansion, label and freeze. To serve, reheat soup slowly, stirring frequently.

■ COOK'S TIP

To chop watercress quickly, trim off the stalks and place the leaves in a food processor. Pulse the blades on and off for 1 minute.

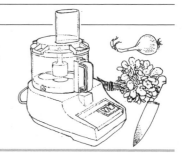

9 BORSCHT

Preparation time:
10 minutes

Cooking time:
1 hour

Serves 6

Calories:
60 per portion

YOU WILL NEED:
450 g/1 lb raw beetroot
2 carrots
1 onion
bay leaf
1.2 litres/2 pints beef stock
salt and pepper
150 ml/¼ pint natural yogurt, to
    garnish

Grate or finely chop the beetroot. Finely chop one carrot and
the onion. Grate the second carrot. Put the vegetables, bay
leaf, stock and seasoning into a saucepan. Bring to the boil,
reduce the heat and simmer for 1 hour. Taste the soup and
adjust the seasoning.

Pour the borscht into individual soup bowls and top each
serving with a spoonful of natural yogurt.

10 MINESTRONE

Preparation time:
25 minutes, plus
overnight soaking

Cooking time:
1 hour 15 minutes

Serves 6

Calories:
220 per portion

YOU WILL NEED:
50 g/2 oz dried haricot beans
1 onion, chopped
1 garlic clove, crushed
2 tablespoons oil
4 rashers rindless bacon, diced
1 × 425 g/15 oz can tomatoes
1.2 litres/2 pints chicken stock
1 leek, cut into rings
2 carrots, diced
¼ small white cabbage, finely
    shredded
salt and pepper
50 g/2 oz pasta shapes
1 tablespoon grated Parmesan cheese,
    to serve

Cover the haricot beans with plenty of cold water and soak
overnight. Drain. Fry the onion and garlic in the oil in a large
saucepan, then add the bacon and continue cooking for a
further few minutes.

Stir in the tomatoes, stock and haricot beans, then bring
to the boil, cover and simmer gently for 45 minutes. Add the
leek, carrot and white cabbage and continue simmering for a
further 15 minutes. Season to taste, add the pasta and cook
for 10 minutes, or until the pasta is tender but firm.

Pour the minestrone into individual soup bowls and
sprinkle each serving with Parmesan cheese.

■ COOK'S TIP

*Traditional borscht contains
shredded cabbage and beef
cubes. Add beef to the soup
with the beetroot. Add
cabbage for the last 15
minutes' cooking time.*

■ COOK'S TIP

*To save on soaking time,
substitute 1 × 425 g/15 oz
can white cannellini beans
for the haricot beans. Add
the drained canned beans to
the soup with the pasta.*

11 CURRIED PARSNIP SOUP

Preparation time:
10 minutes

Cooking time:
25 minutes

Serves 6

Calories:
160 per portion

YOU WILL NEED:
1 onion
2 garlic cloves
675 g/1½ lb parsnips, peeled
1 tart dessert apple, peeled and cored
2 tablespoons oil
1 tablespoon curry powder
40 g/1½ oz flour
1.2 litres/2 pints chicken stock
salt and pepper
150 ml/¼ pint natural yogurt, to garnish

Chop the onion, garlic, parsnips and apple. Heat the oil in a saucepan, add the curry powder, vegetables and apple, cook for 5 minutes. Reduce the heat and stir in the flour. Gradually add the stock, stirring all the time, bring to the boil, season to taste and simmer gently for 20 minutes.

Blend the soup in a liquidizer until smooth. Return the soup to the saucepan, reheat, then pour into individual dishes and garnish each serving with a swirl of yogurt.

12 QUICK APPLE AND CASHEW SOUP

Preparation time:
5 minutes

Cooking time:
10 minutes

Serves 4

Calories:
145 per portion

YOU WILL NEED:
1 onion
100 g/4 oz button mushrooms
100 g/4 oz cashew nuts
600 ml/1 pint apple juice
salt and pepper
¼ teaspoon dried mixed herbs
1 teaspoon yeast extract

Chop the onion and halve the mushrooms. Put all the ingredients into a large saucepan, bring to the boil and reduce the heat to simmer gently for 10 minutes.

Pour the soup into individual soup bowls and serve with warmed French bread.

■ COOK'S TIP

Cook some lightly oiled poppadums under a hot grill until puffed and golden. Do not put the grill pan too near the heat or the poppadums may burn.

■ COOK'S TIP

If you have a garden, then try drying some herbs for the winter. Sage, thyme and tarragon, for example, can be tied in bunches and hung in a cool, dry place.

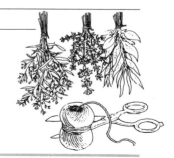

13 MULLIGATAWNY SOUP

Preparation time:
5 minutes

Cooking time:
1 hour

Serves 6

Calories:
145 per portion

YOU WILL NEED:
1 apple
1 large carrot
2 onions
2 tablespoons oil
50 g/2 oz plain flour
1 tablespoon curry powder
1.2 litres/2 pints beef stock
1 tablespoon chutney
50 g/2 oz sultanas
pinch of sugar
salt and pepper
1 teaspoon lemon juice
a few coriander sprigs, to garnish

Dice the apple, carrot and onions. Heat the oil in a saucepan, add the apple and vegetables and cook for 5 minutes. Stir in the flour and curry powder. Gradually pour in the stock, bring to the boil and simmer for 5 minutes. Add the remaining ingredients and simmer together for about 45 minutes to 1 hour.

Blend the soup in a liquidizer until smooth, then return it to the pan to reheat. Taste the soup, adjusting seasoning if necessary, and add a little extra sugar or lemon juice if required.

Garnish with coriander sprigs.

14 CELERY AND STILTON SOUP

Preparation time:
10 minutes

Cooking time:
25-30 minutes

Serves 6

Calories:
290 per portion

YOU WILL NEED:
1 head of celery
1 onion
100 g/4 oz walnuts
50 g/2 oz butter or margarine
50 g/2 oz plain flour
1.2 litres/2 pints chicken stock
salt and pepper
100 g/4 oz blue Stilton cheese
2 tablespoons port (optional)
FOR THE GARNISH
celery curls and leaves, or croûtons

Chop the celery, onion and walnuts. Cook the vegetables in the butter or margarine until softened. Reduce the heat, stir in the walnuts and flour. Gradually add the stock, stirring all the time. Bring to the boil, reduce the heat and simmer gently for 20 minutes.

Season the soup, then transfer it to a liquidizer and blend until smooth. Return the soup to a saucepan and reheat over low heat. Crumble the Stilton and add it to the soup, then stir in the port, if using.

Pour the soup into individual soup bowls and garnish with celery curls and leaves or croûtons.

■ COOK'S TIP

Grind whole spices and use as curry powder. Cinnamon sticks, coriander, cumin and mustard seeds can be combined with ground ginger and chilli powder.

■ MICROWAVE TIP

For croûtons, microwave bread cubes until hard, 3 or 4 minutes, turning often. Melt 40 g/1½ oz butter and mix until butter is absorbed.

15   CHEESE AND ONION SOUP

Preparation time:
10 minutes

Cooking time:
10 minutes

Serves 6

Calories:
490 per portion

YOU WILL NEED:
2 onions
50 g/2 oz butter or margarine
50 g/2 oz plain flour
600 ml/1 pint chicken stock
600 ml/1 pint milk
225 g/8 oz mature Cheddar cheese,
  grated
150 ml/¼ pint dry or medium dry
  cider
¼ teaspoon grated nutmeg
salt and pepper
FOR THE GARNISH
grated cheese
croûtons

Chop the onions and cook in the butter or margarine for 3-5 minutes until soft. Reduce the heat and stir in the flour. Slowly add first the stock, then the milk, stirring all the time. Bring to the boil and cook for 3-4 minutes. Remove the saucepan from the heat, add the Cheddar and stir until all the cheese has melted. Over a low heat, stir in the cider and seasoning. Do not allow the soup to boil.

Pour the soup into individual bowls and garnish with grated cheese and croûtons.

16   FRENCH ONION SOUP

Preparation time:
5 minutes

Cooking time:
25-30 minutes

Serves 6

Calories:
235 per portion

YOU WILL NEED:
450 g/1 lb onions
50 g/2 oz butter or margarine
1 litre/1¾ pints beef stock
150 ml/¼ pint dry red wine
salt and pepper
6 slices French bread, buttered
100 g/4 oz Cheddar cheese, grated

Chop the onions and fry in the butter or margarine until soft and golden brown. Pour in the stock, bring to the boil, then reduce the heat and simmer gently for 25 minutes. Add the wine and seasoning, stir well and heat the soup for a further few minutes.

Put a slice of French bread into each heatproof soup bowl and pour over the soup. When the bread rises to the surface sprinkle the top with the Cheddar, put under a hot grill until golden. Serve immediately.

◼ COOK'S TIP

To chop a peeled onion, cut it in half lengthways; place the flat side on a chopping board. Holding opposite sides, slice finely lengthways, then across.

◼ COOK'S TIP

Coarsely grate and freeze small leftover pieces of cheese – they are often useful for recipes such as this one. Pack the cheese in polythene bags, allowing plenty of room in the bag so that the cheese does not become compressed in a lump. Use straight from the freezer.

17 MUSHROOM AND SHERRY SOUP

Preparation time:
10 minutes

Cooking time:
20 minutes

Serves 6

Calories:
170 per portion

YOU WILL NEED:
450 g/1 lb button mushrooms
1 onion, chopped
2 garlic cloves, crushed
50 g/2 oz butter or margarine
50 g/2 oz plain flour
300 ml/½ pint milk
600 ml/1 pint chicken stock
2 tablespoons sherry
salt and pepper
FOR THE GARNISH
150 ml/¼ pint single cream
1 tablespoon chopped parsley

Thinly slice the mushrooms. In a saucepan, cook the onion and garlic in the butter or margarine until softened. Add the mushrooms and cook gently for a few minutes. Stir in the flour. Gradually blend in the milk and stock. Bring to the boil, reduce the heat and simmer gently for 15 minutes. Stir the soup frequently to ensure a smooth consistency.

Add the sherry and season to taste. Pour into soup bowls. Garnish the soup with a swirl of cream and sprinkle with parsley.

18 COCK-A-LEEKIE SOUP

Preparation time:
10 minutes

Cooking time:
1 hour

Serves 6

Calories:
100 per portion

YOU WILL NEED:
1 chicken carcass
1 onion
bouquet garni
1.2 litres/2 pints chicken stock
about 100 g/4 oz cooked chicken
3 carrots
450 g/1 lb leeks
100 g/4 oz no-need-to-soak prunes
salt and pepper
1 tablespoon chopped parsley, to garnish

Simmer the chicken carcass, onion and bouquet garni in the stock for an hour, then strain the liquid into a large saucepan.

Slice the chicken meat into strips. Thinly slice the carrots and leeks. Add the chicken, vegetables and prunes to the stock. Bring to the boil and simmer gently for 20 minutes. Season with salt and pepper.

Serve the soup garnished with freshly chopped parsley.

■ COOK'S TIP

For a low-calorie soup, omit onion, butter and flour. Simmer mushrooms in 900 ml/1½ pints stock. Add chopped spring onions and sherry. Omit milk and cream.

■ COOK'S TIP

To chop a small amount of parsley, place a few parsley sprigs in a large cup or mug and snip with scissors, turning the cup with one hand.

19 CREAM OF CHICKEN SOUP

Preparation time:
5 minutes

Cooking time:
1 hour 10 minutes

Serves 6

Calories:
165 per portion

YOU WILL NEED:
1 chicken carcass
1 onion
bouquet garni
1.2 litres/2 pints chicken stock
about 100 g/4 oz cooked chicken
300 ml/½ pint milk
50 g/2 oz plain flour
2 tablespoons water
1 tablespoon lemon juice
¼ teaspoon grated nutmeg
salt and pepper
150 ml/¼ pint single cream
croûtons, to garnish

Simmer the carcass, onion and bouquet garni in the stock for an hour. Strain the liquid, return to the saucepan.

Neatly dice the cooked chicken meat. Add the chicken meat and milk to the stock. Blend the flour with the water, then slowly add the mixture to the stock, stirring all the time. Bring to the boil, reduce the heat and simmer gently for 10 minutes. Season the soup with lemon juice, nutmeg, salt and pepper.

Stir in the cream, pour the soup into individual soup bowls and garnish with croûtons.

20 SCOTCH BROTH

Preparation time:
10 minutes

Cooking time:
2½ hours

Serves 6

Calories:
110 per portion

YOU WILL NEED:
50 g/2 oz pearl barley
225 g/8 oz neck of mutton or lamb, or stewing beef
2 leeks
2 carrots
1 onion
2 celery sticks
1 small turnip
1.2 litres/2 pints water
bouquet garni
salt and pepper
1 tablespoon chopped parsley, to garnish

Blanch the pearl barley in boiling water for 3 minutes, then strain. Cut the meat into small cubes. Slice the leeks, carrots, onion and celery. Dice the turnip.

Bring the water, pearl barley, meat, bouquet garni and seasoning to taste slowly to the boil in a saucepan. Skim. Reduce the heat, add the vegetables and simmer gently for 1½ hours, skimming off any foam that may appear on the surface of the broth. Remove the bouquet garni.

Pour the broth into individual soup bowls and garnish each serving with chopped parsley.

COOK'S TIP

Instead of small square croûtons, use cocktail cutters or small biscuit cutters to make attractive shapes.

COOK'S TIP

For a fresh bouquet garni, tie a sprig each of parsley and thyme and a bay leaf together. Tie to the saucepan handle so it can be removed easily.

21 BEEF SOUP WITH DUMPLINGS

Preparation time:
15 minutes

Cooking time:
1 hour 20 minutes

Serves 6

Calories:
340 per portion

YOU WILL NEED:
450 g/1 lb braising steak, cubed
25 g/1 oz plain flour
50 g/2 oz butter or margarine
2 onions, finely chopped
2 garlic cloves, crushed
1 teaspoon marjoram
1 teaspoon paprika
salt and pepper
1.2 litres/2 pints beef stock
FOR THE DUMPLINGS
2 day-old bread rolls
6 tablespoons lukewarm milk
1 onion, finely chopped
1 tablespoon oil
2 tablespoons chopped parsley
1 egg

Coat the beef in flour. Melt the fat in a large saucepan, add the onion and garlic and fry for 3 minutes. Add the meat and fry until browned on all sides. Add the marjoram and seasoning. Gradually blend in the stock, bring to the boil, reduce the heat and simmer for 1 hour. Cut the rolls into thin slices and soften with the warmed milk. Cook the onion in the oil. Mix together the bread, onion, parsley, seasoning and egg. With wet hands, form the mixture into six small balls.

Add the dumplings to the soup and simmer for a further 15 minutes. Serve each portion of soup with a dumpling.

22 BACON AND SPLIT PEA SOUP

Preparation time:
10 minutes, plus overnight soaking

Cooking time:
1 hour 10 minutes

Serves 6

Calories:
295 per portion

YOU WILL NEED:
100 g/4 oz split peas
1 small turnip
1 carrot
2 leeks
2 tablespoons oil
8 rashers rindless smoked streaky bacon, diced
1.5 litres/2½ pints ham or chicken stock
salt and pepper
½ teaspoon dried mixed herbs
150 ml/¼ pint single cream
1 tablespoon chopped parsley, to garnish

Cover the split peas with cold water and soak them overnight. Drain well. Dice the turnip and carrot. Slice the leeks into rings.

Cook the vegetables in the oil for 5 minutes, add the bacon and continue cooking for a few minutes. Add the stock and split peas. Season well with salt, pepper and the mixed herbs. Simmer gently for an hour. Blend the soup in a liquidizer until smooth.

Return the soup to the saucepan and reheat over a low heat. Stir in the cream. Pour into individual soup bowls and garnish each serving with chopped parsley.

■ FREEZER TIP

Cool soup quickly and freeze. Freeze dumplings separately. To reheat, bring soup to the boil, add defrosted dumplings, and cook as above.

■ COOK'S TIP

Reserve the cooking liquid from a joint of bacon for this soup. Omit the streaky bacon. Cool and chill the liquid, then skim off any fat before use.

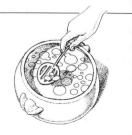

23   SEAFOOD SOUP

Preparation time:
15 minutes

Cooking time:
30 minutes

Serves 6

Calories:
245 per portion

YOU WILL NEED:
600 ml/1 pint water
350 g/12 oz haddock
1 bay leaf
1 lemon, cut into wedges
salt and pepper
1 onion, chopped
2 garlic cloves, crushed
1 tablespoon oil
25 g/1 oz plain flour
600 ml/1 pint milk
350 g/12 oz cooked peeled prawns and
   bottled mussels (mixed)
¼ teaspoon ground mace
2 tablespoons lemon juice
2 tablespoons dry white wine
   (optional)
4 tablespoons single cream
croûtons, to garnish

Bring the water, haddock, bay leaf, lemon wedges and season-ing to the boil and simmer gently for 15 minutes. Drain the fish, reserving the cooking liquid. Discard the bay leaf and lemon wedges. Skin, bone and flake the fish.

In a large saucepan, cook the onion and garlic in the oil until softened. Reduce the heat, add the flour, then gradually pour in the milk, stirring all the time. Add the seafood, mace, lemon juice, wine (if using) and seasoning to taste, simmer for 5 minutes, then add the fish and simmer for a further 5 minutes. Remove from heat. Stir in the cream. Garnish each serving with croûtons.

24   WHITE FISH CHOWDER

Preparation time:
10 minutes

Cooking time:
25-30 minutes

Serves 6

Calories:
295 per portion

YOU WILL NEED:
2 rashers rindless bacon
450 g/1 lb coley, haddock or cod
50 g/2 oz butter or margarine
4 medium potatoes, peeled and diced
2 leeks, sliced into rings
50 g/2 oz button mushrooms
600 ml/1 pint milk
salt and pepper
pinch of grated nutmeg
1 × 227g/8 oz can tomatoes
1 tablespoon chopped parsley, to
   garnish

Dice the bacon and fry in its own fat until crisp; remove from the pan. Cut the fish into small pieces, removing skin and bones.

Heat the butter or margarine in a saucepan, then add the fish, potato, leek and mushrooms. Cook for 2 minutes. Add the milk, then simmer gently for 15-20 minutes. Season with salt and pepper and the nutmeg. Stir in the bacon and toma-toes and heat through gently.

Pour the chowder into individual soup bowls and garnish with freshly chopped parsley.

■ COOK'S TIP

Mace is the outer covering of the nutmeg. It is used to season savoury dishes like pâtés, baked meats and soups.

■ FREEZER TIP

Frozen cod steaks are ideal for this chowder. Defrost for about 15 minutes, then cut into cubes and cook while still partially frozen.

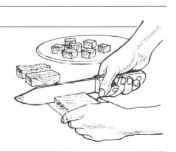

STARTERS & SNACKS

A starter should be light, well-flavoured and provide a contrast in texture and flavour to the courses which follow. A well chosen starter should whet the appetite for the meal, not blunt it. Many of the recipes in this chapter are also suitable to serve for a snack lunch or supper, whilst later recipes are for more substantial snacks.

25 RICH TUNA MOUSSE

Preparation time:
25 minutes

Cooking time:
25 minutes, plus 1 hour to set

Serves 4

Calories:
880 per portion

YOU WILL NEED:
1 onion
2 × 198 g/7 oz cans tuna
50 g/2 oz butter
3 tablespoons dry white wine
1 tablespoon gelatine
3 tablespoons boiling water
1 teaspoon horseradish sauce
300 ml/½ pint mayonnaise
6 tablespoons double cream
salt and pepper
lime slices, to garnish

Finely chop the onion. Drain and flake the tuna. Beat the butter until creamy. Blend the onion, fish and butter together with a fork.

Pour the wine into a bowl. Sprinkle in the gelatine, then pour in the boiling water, stand over a pan of simmering water and stir until the gelatine has dissolved. Cool the mixture slightly. Blend in the horseradish and mayonnaise. Put the tuna mixture in a liquidizer, add the gelatine mixture and blend until smooth.

In a bowl, beat the cream until stiff. Fold the fish mixture into the cream and season to taste. Turn the mousse into individual ramekins.

Refrigerate for about 1 hour, until set.

Garnish each serving with a twist of lime and serve with brown bread or vegetable crudités.

26 SMOKED HADDOCK PATE

Preparation time:
10 minutes

Cooking time:
20 minutes

Oven temperature:
200 C, 400 F, gas 6

Serves 4

Calories:
165 per portion

YOU WILL NEED:
2 large fillets smoked haddock, cooked
2 hard-boiled eggs
75 g/3 oz wholemeal breadcrumbs
1 thick slice onion, finely chopped
150 ml/¼ pint natural yogurt
salt and pepper
1 tablespoon chopped parsley
1 tablespoon grated lemon rind
lemon slices, to garnish

Finely flake the fish. Finely chop the hard-boiled eggs. Mix together the fish, eggs, breadcrumbs, onion and yogurt. Beat until smooth. Season with salt and pepper, then fold in the parsley and lemon rind.

Spoon the mixture into four individual ramekins. Smooth the top of the pâté with the back of a teaspoon, then bake in a moderately hot oven for 20 minutes.

Garnish the pâté with lemon twists and serve immediately with triangles of hot toast.

Variation
This dish can also be served cold. Follow the recipe above, but chill the pâté for an hour before serving. Serve with brown bread and butter.

■ COOK'S TIP

For crudités, prepare matchstick carrots, tiny cauliflower florets, celery sticks, button mushrooms, strips of pepper and scrubbed radishes.

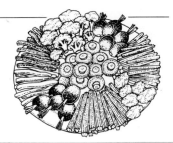

■ COOK'S TIP

If you want just one slice of onion, cut it off the whole unpeeled onion. Wrap the remainder in cling film. It will keep in the refrigerator for up to a week.

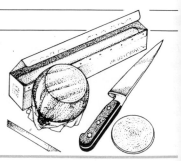

27 POTTED PRAWNS

Preparation time:
20 minutes, plus 30 minutes to chill

Cooking time:
5 minutes

Serves 4

Calories:
555 per portion

YOU WILL NEED:
4 spring onions
450 g/1 lb peeled cooked prawns
150 ml/¼ pint mayonnaise
2 teaspoons horseradish sauce
2 tablespoons lemon juice
pinch of cayenne
salt and pepper
100 g/4 oz butter
FOR THE GARNISH
whole prawns
watercress sprigs
curly endive (optional)

Thinly slice the spring onions. Place 225 g/8 oz prawns in a liquidizer, add the mayonnaise, horseradish, spring onions and lemon juice. Blend the mixture to a paste. Mix the remaining prawns into the paste. Add the cayenne, salt and pepper. Press the prawn mixture into individual ramekins.

Melt the butter in a small saucepan, then pour it over the potted prawns, dividing the quantity evenly between the ramekins. Refrigerate until the butter is firm, about 30 minutes.

Garnish the potted prawns with whole prawns, watercress and curly endive, if liked, and serve with hot buttered toast.

28 QUICK TARAMASALATA

Preparation time:
10 minutes, plus 1 hour to chill

Serves 4

Calories:
305 per portion

YOU WILL NEED:
100 g/4 oz smoked cod's roe
75 g/3 oz fresh white bread
2 tablespoons milk
1 large garlic clove, crushed
100 ml/4 fl oz olive oil
juice of ½ lemon
FOR THE GARNISH
lemon slices
parsley sprigs

To retain pink flecks, skin the roe rather than scoop out the middle. Trim the crusts from the bread and soak the slices in the milk for 15 minutes, remove and squeeze dry. Mash with the cod's roe and crushed garlic.

Place the mixture in a liquidizer. Pour in the oil gradually, while blending, then add the lemon juice and blend until smooth. Chill for an hour before serving.

Garnish with lemon slices and parsley sprigs and serve the taramasalata with a selection of packeted savoury snacks and a green salad.

◼ MICROWAVE TIP

To defrost prawns, lay on two sheets of absorbent kitchen paper. Cover with more paper and cook on full power for about 3 minutes (for 450 g/1 lb).

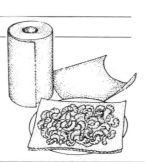

◼ COOK'S TIP

Serve stoned black olives and warm pitta bread with the taramasalata. To stone olives quickly use a cherry stoner.

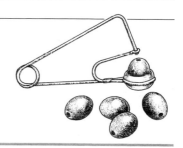

29 CHICKEN LIVER PATE

Preparation time:
20 minutes

Cooking time:
15 minutes, plus 2
hours to chill

Serves 6

Calories:
280 per portion

YOU WILL NEED:
1 onion
1 garlic clove
1 tablespoon oil
*450 g/1 lb chicken or turkey livers,
    trimmed*
100 g/4 oz butter
salt and pepper
pinch of grated nutmeg
1 teaspoon mixed herbs
2 tablespoons dry sherry
2 tablespoons double cream

Line and grease a 450 g/1 lb loaf tin. Finely chop the onion
and garlic. In a saucepan cook the onion and garlic in the oil
until softened. Add the chicken or turkey livers, cover the pan
and cook over low heat for 10 minutes. Cool slightly, then
blend the mixture in a liquidizer until smooth.

Melt the butter in the saucepan already used. Add the
seasonings, mixed herbs, sherry and cream. When heated
through, add the mixture to the liver purée and blend until the
consistency is of whipped cream. Pour the purée into the prepared tin and chill, covered, for 2 hours or more.

To serve, turn out the pâté on to a serving plate and remove paper. Accompany each serving with a fresh tomato
and Chinese leaves, or a small side salad and melba toast.

30 SALAD NICOISE

Preparation time:
15 minutes

Serves 4

Calories:
270 per portion

YOU WILL NEED:
a few lettuce leaves
1 × 198 g/7 oz can tuna
1 green pepper, seeded
1 onion
2 tomatoes
2 hard-boiled eggs
100 g/4 oz French beans, cooked
*4 tablespoons French dressing (recipe
    125)*
salt and pepper
FOR THE GARNISH
1 × 50 g/2 oz can anchovy fillets
a few black olives, halved and stoned

Arrange the lettuce leaves on four small plates. Drain the tuna
and break it into chunks with a fork. Cut the pepper into
strips. Thinly slice the onion into rings. Quarter the tomatoes
and eggs.

Lightly toss all the ingredients together in the French
dressing, then season to taste.

Spoon the salad over the lettuce leaves and garnish with
the anchovy fillets and black olives. Serve with hot French
bread.

■ COOK'S TIP

*For melba toast, cut crusts
off medium-thick sliced
bread. Lightly toast on both
sides. Slice horizontally,
then toast the second side of
each thin piece.*

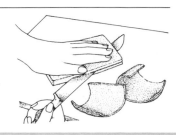

■ COOK'S TIP

*To prevent black rings
forming around the yolks of
hard-boiled eggs, drain and
leave in the saucepan under
a running cold tap for about
2 minutes.*

31 EGGS MAYONNAISE

Preparation time:
15 minutes

Cooking time:
10 minutes

Serves 4

Calories:
230 per portion

YOU WILL NEED:
4 eggs
4 tablespoons mayonnaise
3 tablespoons double cream or
   whipping cream
2 teaspoons lemon juice
¼ teaspoon paprika
salt
8 lettuce leaves
1 tablespoon freshly chopped chives,
   to garnish

Hard-boil the eggs for 10 minutes, then plunge them into cold water at once to prevent a dark line forming around the yolk. Leave the eggs to cool. Remove the shells and halve the eggs lengthways.

Mix together the mayonnaise, cream, lemon juice and seasoning. Arrange two lettuce leaves on each of four individual serving plates. Top the lettuce with two egg halves. Pour the mayonnaise mixture over the egg halves.

Garnish each serving with a sprinkle of chopped chives and serve with brown bread and butter.

32 STUFFED MUSHROOMS

Preparation time:
15 minutes

Cooking time:
30 minutes

Oven temperature:
180 C, 350 F, gas 4

Serves 4

Calories:
295 per portion

YOU WILL NEED:
12 large mushrooms
1 garlic clove, crushed
1 onion, finely chopped
50 g/2 oz butter
3 tablespoons oil
50 g/2 oz fresh breadcrumbs
50 g/2 oz Parmesan cheese, grated
salt and pepper
FOR THE GARNISH
tomato wedges
watercress sprigs

Remove the stems from the mushrooms and chop the stems finely. In a small saucepan, cook the garlic and onions in 25 g/1 oz of the butter and 1 tablespoon of the oil until soft. Add the chopped mushroom stems and stir over a moderate heat for about 5 minutes. Remove from the heat. Mix in the remaining oil, the breadcrumbs and Parmesan. Season to taste.

Stuff the mushroom tops with the mixture. Top each cap with a dot of the remaining butter.

Arrange the mushrooms in a shallow well-oiled ovenproof dish and bake in a moderate oven for about 25 minutes. Serve hot, garnished with tomato wedges and watercress sprigs.

■ COOK'S TIP

To make spicy egg mayonnaise, add 2 teaspoons of curry powder to the mayonnaise mixture and garnish with parsley sprigs and lemon slices.

■ MICROWAVE TIP

Microwave onion and garlic on full power 4 minutes. Add mushroom stems and cook 2 minutes. Cook filled mushrooms in two batches on full power 3-4 minutes.

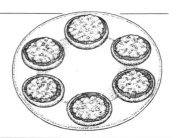

33 INDIVIDUAL ONION QUICHES

Preparation time:
20 minutes

Cooking time:
35 minutes

Oven temperature:
200 C, 400 F, gas 6

Serves 4

Calories:
625 per portion

YOU WILL NEED:
225 g/8 oz plain flour
pinch of salt
100 g/4 oz margarine
2 tablespoons cold water
FOR THE FILLING
2 large onions, sliced into rings
2 tablespoons oil
2 eggs
150 ml/¼ pint milk
salt and pepper
100 g/4 oz Cheddar cheese, grated
FOR THE GARNISH
onion rings (optional)
coriander sprigs (optional)

Sift the flour and salt into a mixing bowl. Rub in the fat until the mixture resembles fine breadcrumbs. Gradually add the water and form the mixture into a ball. Put the pastry on a lightly floured board. Roll it out and use to line four 11 cm/4½ inch quiche rings or flan dishes.

Cook the onion rings in the oil until soft. Beat the eggs lightly, then beat in the milk, season and add the cheese. Divide the onions equally amongst the quiches. Pour over the egg mixture.

Bake the quiches in a moderately hot oven for 30 minutes.

34 AVOCADO DIP

Preparation time:
10 minutes, plus 15 minutes to chill

Serves 4

Calories:
130 per portion

YOU WILL NEED:
1 onion
1 green chilli
1 tomato
2 avocados
juice of 1 lemon
1 or 2 garlic cloves, crushed
salt and pepper

Finely chop the onion. Slit, seed, rinse, dry and finely chop the green chilli. Peel, seed and chop the tomato.

Peel and stone the avocados. Mash to a chunky consistency in a bowl. Add the lemon juice, onion, garlic and chilli. Mix thoroughly, then season to taste with salt and pepper. Stir in the chopped tomato, then transfer the dip to a serving bowl or four individual bowls.

Chill for at least 15 minutes. Serve with taco chips, salted crisps, or vegetable crudités.

■ FREEZER TIP

Place the cooled quiches on a baking tray, covered with cling film. Freeze until hard, then pack into polythene bags, seal, and return to the freezer. Use within 1 month.

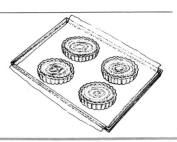

■ COOK'S TIP

Wash your hands well after handling chillies and do not rub your eyes when cutting them. Remove the hot seeds and rinse the chillies under cold running water.

35 GRILLED GRAPEFRUIT

Preparation time:
5 minutes, plus 10
minutes standing
time

Cooking time:
5 minutes

Serves 4

Calories:
85 per portion

YOU WILL NEED:
2 grapefruit
50 g/2 oz brown sugar
2 tablespoons rum, brandy or
vermouth
few sprigs mint, to garnish

Halve the grapefruit, loosen the segments from the skin and
from the centre with a grapefruit knife or other sharp knife,
so they are easy to remove. Sprinkle each half with sugar.
Pour over the rum, brandy or vermouth. Leave to stand for 10
minutes to allow the sugar and alcohol to soak right through
the grapefruit.

Cook the grapefruit halves under a hot grill for about 5
minutes. Serve this starter immediately garnished with a sprig
of fresh mint.

36 MELON AND BLACK GRAPE COCKTAIL

Preparation time:
10 minutes, plus 1
hour to chill

Serves 4

Calories:
50 per portion

YOU WILL NEED:
1 small honeydew melon
225 g/8 oz black grapes
2 teaspoons mint sauce
1 teaspoon caster sugar
few sprigs mint, to garnish

Halve the honeydew melon and scoop out the seeds. Use a
melon baller to remove the fruit in neat balls into a bowl.
Halve and remove the seeds from the black grapes. Add the
grape halves to the melon, then add the mint sauce and sugar.

Cover the cocktail and chill for about an hour, tossing
occasionally. Check the flavour, adding a little more sugar if
required.

Serve the cocktail in glasses and garnish them with sprigs
of fresh mint.

■ COOK'S TIP

Using a sharp pointed knife,
cut around the middle of
the grapefruit in towards
the centre in a zig-zag
pattern. Pull the halves
apart gently.

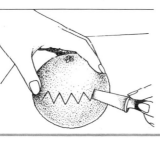

■ COOK'S TIP

For special occasions, frost
the tops of the glasses by
dipping the rims lightly in
beaten egg white then sugar.

37 TOASTED SANDWICHES

Preparation time:
10-15 minutes

Each filling makes 3

Calories:
276 per sandwich
with Filling 1
236 per sandwich
with Filling 2

YOU WILL NEED:
12 slices bread
50 g/2 oz butter or margarine
watercress sprigs, to garnish
FILLING 1
3 slices cooked ham
50 g/2 oz Cheddar cheese, grated
salt and pepper
FILLING 2
1 × 120 g/4¼ oz can sardines in
*   tomato sauce*
2 slices onion, finely chopped
salt and pepper

Remove and discard the crusts from the bread. Butter each slice. For filling 1, place a slice of ham on the unbuttered side of each of three slices of bread. Sprinkle with cheese and seasoning, then cover with second slices of bread, buttered side out, place in a sandwich toaster and cook for 5 minutes, or until crisp and golden.

For filling 2, remove the bones and mash the sardines. Spread the sardines on the unbuttered side of each of three slices of bread, sprinkle the onion on top, season and cover with second slices of bread, buttered side out, and toast as above.

Garnish with watercress sprigs and serve with celery sticks and tomatoes.

38 SPEEDY PIZZAS

Preparation time:
10 minutes

Cooking time:
20-25 minutes

Serves 4

Calories:
530 per portion

YOU WILL NEED:
1 small French loaf
50 g/2 oz butter
1 onion, finely chopped
1 garlic clove, crushed
1 tablespoon oil
100 g/4 oz button mushrooms
1 × 425 g/15 oz can tomatoes
100 g/4 oz mozzarella cheese
100 g/4 oz Cheddar cheese
salt and pepper
¼ teaspoon oregano

Cut the French loaf in half horizontally and butter each half. Cut each half across the middle so that you have four pieces of bread.

Cook the onion and garlic in the oil until soft. Add the mushrooms and cook for a few minutes, then add the tomatoes. Simmer vigorously for 10 minutes or until the tomato is reduced and thickened. Meanwhile dice the cheeses into small pieces.

Spread the French sticks with the tomato mixture, sprinkle over salt, pepper and the oregano. Dot the cheese evenly on the top (be careful not to put it too near the edges).

Brown under the grill for 5-10 minutes, or until the cheese has melted and the pizzas are heated through.

■ COOK'S TIP

If you do not have a sandwich toaster, brown the sandwiches both sides under a hot grill. Or quickly shallow fry them. Drain on absorbent kitchen paper.

■ MICROWAVE TIP

Instead of browning them under the grill, halve the pizzas and cook on full power in the microwave for about 5 minutes, until heated through.

39 WELSH RAREBIT

Preparation time:
5 minutes

Cooking time:
8-10 minutes

Serves 4

Calories:
390 per portion

YOU WILL NEED:
225 g/8 oz Cheddar cheese
25 g/1 oz butter
25 g/1 oz plain flour
salt and pepper
pinch of cayenne
pinch of mustard powder
150 ml/¼ pint milk or beer
few drops of Worcestershire sauce
4 slices bread
butter for spreading

Grate the cheese. Melt the butter in a saucepan, reduce the heat, add the cheese, flour, seasonings, milk or beer and Worcestershire sauce. Heat the mixture gently, stirring occasionally, until a smooth, thick sauce is formed.

Toast and butter the bread. Top with the cheese mixture and brown under the grill for 2-3 minutes.

Serve immediately with grilled tomatoes, or garnished with tomato wedges and a coriander sprig.

40 COCKTAIL KEBABS

Preparation time:
15-20 minutes

Cooking time:
20-25 minutes

Makes 16

Calories:
230 per portion

YOU WILL NEED:
1 onion, finely chopped
1 tablespoon oil
1 × 227g/8 oz can tomatoes
2 teaspoons tomato ketchup
½ teaspoon chilli powder
few drops of Worcestershire sauce
salt and pepper
8 rashers rindless bacon, halved
8 cocktail sausages
4 large cubes of pineapple
4 stuffed green olives

First make the spicy dip: cook the onion in the oil until softened, add the tomatoes and bring to the boil. Add the tomato ketchup, chilli powder, Worcestershire sauce and seasoning. Simmer gently for 5-10 minutes, or until reduced. Blend the mixture in a liquidizer until smooth, then pour it into a small serving bowl.

Pleat four halved bacon rashers on to a metal skewer. Wrap the remaining rashers around the sausages and the pineapple cubes and thread on to metal skewers.

Cook the kebabs under a hot grill for 10-15 minutes. Use a metal fork to slide the cooked ingredients off the metal skewers on to a double-thick piece of absorbent kitchen paper. Mop any excess fat off the top with another piece of absorbent kitchen paper. Thread the bacon on to wooden cocktail sticks with the olives. Thread the sausages on sticks with the pineapple. Arrange the cocktail kebabs in a serving dish and serve with the dip.

■ COOK'S TIP

Make satisfying and tasty buck rarebit by topping the Welsh rarebit with a poached egg. Add roughly chopped parsley for colour.

■ COOK'S TIP

To remove items from skewers, use the prongs of a fork. Remember to protect your hand with a double-thick tea-towel if the skewers are hot.

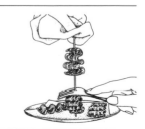

FISH DISHES

Delicious, nutritious, low in calories, and quick to cook, fish is a near-perfect food. These recipes include all the popular fresh fish as well as making use of ready-prepared canned and frozen fish.

41 FISH KEBABS

Preparation time:
15 minutes, plus 1 hour to marinate

Cooking time:
12 minutes

Serves 4

Calories:
300 per portion

YOU WILL NEED:
4 frozen cod or coley steaks, defrosted
1 large green pepper, seeded
100 g/4 oz button mushrooms
8 bay leaves
4 tablespoons olive oil
2 garlic cloves, crushed
1 tablespoon lemon juice
salt and pepper
1 teaspoon dill weed
1 × 340 g/12 oz can pineapple chunks, drained
2 kiwi fruit, peeled and quartered
1 × 410 g/14½ oz can apricot halves, drained

Cut the fish steaks into 2.5 cm/1 inch cubes. Cut the pepper into 2.5 cm/1 inch squares. Wipe the mushrooms. Place the fish, pepper, mushrooms and bay leaves in a glass dish. Mix together the oil, garlic, lemon juice, salt and pepper and dill weed and pour over the fish mixture. Cover and chill for an hour, then remove the kebab ingredients, reserving the marinade.

Thread the peppers, pineapple, fish, bay leaves, kiwi fruit, mushrooms and apricots on to the skewers, continuing until all the ingredients have been used up.

Heat the grill to medium heat. Place the kebabs on a rack in the grill pan, and cook for 12 minutes, turning the kebabs as necessary and basting frequently with the marinade. Serve with Saffron Rice (recipe 149).

42 GRILLED COD STEAKS WITH PARSLEY BUTTER

Preparation time:
10 minutes

Cooking time:
12-16 minutes

Serves 4

Calories:
270 per portion

YOU WILL NEED:
4 fresh cod steaks
salt and pepper
100 g/4 oz butter
1 tablespoon chopped parsley
1 tablespoon lemon juice
FOR THE GARNISH
lemon wedges
coriander sprig (optional)

Season the fish generously with salt and pepper on each side. Cover and chill while preparing the parsley butter.

Beat the butter until soft and creamy. Work in the parsley, lemon juice and seasoning to taste. Using half the butter spread a little over each side of each fish steak.

Turn the grill on to medium heat. Place the cod steaks on a sheet of foil and grill for 6-8 minutes on each side or until the fish is cooked through.

Top the cod steaks with the remaining parsley butter and garnish with lemon wedges and a coriander sprig, if liked. Serve at once.

■ COOK'S TIP

Saffron strands should be pounded to a powder in a pestle and mortar. Add a little hot water to extract the maximum colour and flavour.

■ MICROWAVE TIP

Microwave chilled butter on full power for about 15-30 seconds to soften. Defrost frozen butter for 45-60 seconds – remove foiled wrapping first.

43 FISH AU GRATIN

Preparation time:
15 minutes

Cooking time:
12-16 minutes

Serves 4

Calories:
205 per portion

YOU WILL NEED:
50 g/2 oz fresh white breadcrumbs
4 fresh cod steaks
salt and pepper
25 g/1 oz butter or margarine
50 g/2 oz Cheddar cheese, grated
¼ teaspoon mustard powder
lemon twists, to garnish

Spread the breadcrumbs on a sheet of foil and grill until golden and crunchy, then leave to cool.

Season the cod steaks generously with salt and pepper on each side. Dot the butter or margarine over one side of the fish. Turn the grill on to medium heat. Place the cod steaks buttered side up on a sheet of foil and grill for 6-8 minutes. Turn them over, mix together the breadcrumbs, cheese, mustard and seasoning to taste, sprinkle over the fish and grill for a further 6-8 minutes.

Place the cod steaks in a hot serving dish, garnish with lemon twists and serve at once with jacket potatoes and a green vegetable.

44 HADDOCK IN CIDER

Preparation time:
20 minutes

Cooking time:
30 minutes

Oven temperature:
180 C, 350 F, gas 4

Serves 4

Calories:
320 per portion

YOU WILL NEED:
10 shallots, peeled
100 g/4 oz button mushrooms
1-2 tablespoons oil
2 celery sticks, thinly sliced
1 green pepper, seeded and diced
4 fresh haddock steaks
salt and pepper
300 ml/½ pint dry cider
25 g/1 oz butter or margarine
25 g/1 oz plain flour
150 ml/¼ pint single cream
chopped parsley, to garnish

Fry the shallots and mushrooms in the oil until golden. Transfer to a casserole dish. Add the celery and pepper to the pan and cook for a few minutes. Add to the casserole. Place the haddock steaks in the casserole, season with salt and pepper. Pour over the cider and bake in a moderate oven for 25 minutes or until the fish flakes easily when tested with the point of a knife. Transfer the fish and vegetables to a serving plate, cover and keep warm. Carefully drain off the cooking liquor. Melt the butter or margarine in a small saucepan, add the flour, then gradually add the cooking liquor, stirring continuously. Bring the sauce to the boil, season to taste, reduce the heat and simmer gently for 1-2 minutes. Stir in the cream and reheat without boiling. Pour the sauce over the fish, garnish with chopped parsley and serve immediately.

■ COOK'S TIP

A quick way to make breadcrumbs: take a large piece of bread and rub it on the coarse side of a grater.

■ COOK'S TIP

To avoid runny eyes when peeling shallots or pickling onions, peel them in a bowl of water. Drain and discard the skin when all are peeled.

45 HADDOCK CRUMBLE

Preparation time:
20 minutes

Cooking time:
30 minutes

Oven temperature:
200 C, 400 F, gas 6

Serves 4

Calories:
740 per portion

YOU WILL NEED:
675 g/1½ lb haddock fillets
6 tablespoons water
salt and pepper
FOR THE SAUCE
1 small onion, chopped
50 g/2 oz butter
40 g/1½ oz plain flour
600 ml/1 pint milk
juice of ½ lemon
50 g/2 oz Cheddar cheese, grated
FOR THE TOPPING
50 g/2 oz butter or margarine
100 g/4 oz plain flour
50 g/2 oz jumbo oats
1 tablespoon chopped fresh dill
knob of butter
dill sprig, to garnish

Put the haddock, water and seasoning in a pan. Cover and poach for 5 minutes. Reserve any liquor and flake the fish, discarding skin. Fry onion in butter for 3 minutes, then add the flour. Gradually stir in the milk. Bring the sauce to the boil, add the lemon juice, seasoning and strained fish liquor. Simmer for 2 minutes. Add the cheese and fish to the sauce, then pour into an ovenproof dish.

Rub the fat into the flour until the mixture resembles fine breadcrumbs. Stir in oats, dill and seasoning. Spread on top of the fish. Dot with butter and bake in a moderately hot oven for 30 minutes or until golden. Garnish with dill.

46 PLAICE VERONIQUE

Preparation time:
10 minutes

Cooking time:
15 minutes

Oven temperature:
190 C, 375 F, gas 5

Serves 4

Calories:
315 per portion

YOU WILL NEED:
8 medium plaice fillets, skinned
salt and pepper
150 ml/¼ pint dry white wine
1 tablespoon lemon juice
100 g/4 oz seedless grapes, plus a few extra to garnish (optional)
25 g/1 oz butter or margarine
25 g/1 oz plain flour
150 ml/¼ pint milk

Roll up each fillet skinned side inwards. Place the fish rolls in a greased ovenproof dish. Season the fish with salt and pepper, pour over the wine and lemon juice. Cover and bake in a moderately hot oven for about 15 minutes, or until the fish flakes easily when tested with the point of a knife. Transfer the fish to a serving dish and keep warm. Reserve the cooking liquor for the sauce.

Place the grapes in boiling water, boil for 1 minute, then drain. Heat the butter or margarine over a gentle heat, add the flour, then gradually add the milk, seasoning and reserved cooking liquor, stirring continuously. Bring the sauce to the boil, reduce the heat and simmer gently for 2 minutes, stirring occasionally. Pour the sauce over the fish and garnish with the grapes adding a few unblanched grapes if you like. Serve at once.

■ COOK'S TIP

To skin fish fillets, place skin side down. Hold tail end. With a sharp knife cut at an acute angle, using a sawing motion between flesh and skin.

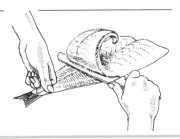

■ MICROWAVE TIP

Put the rolls on a dish. Cover and microwave 5 minutes on full power. Mix in remaining ingredients, cover and cook 5 minutes. Add grapes, cook 1 minute.

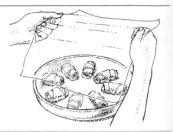

47 STUFFED PLAICE ROLLS

Preparation time:
20 minutes

Cooking time:
20-25 minutes

Oven temperature:
180 C, 350 F, gas 4

Serves 4

Calories:
390 per portion

YOU WILL NEED:
8 small plaice fillets, skinned
100 g/4 oz white breadcrumbs
grated rind and juice of 1 lemon
1 tablespoon chopped fresh dill
50 g/2 oz cream cheese
salt and pepper
1 egg, lightly beaten
25 g/1 oz butter or margarine
25 g/1 oz plain flour
300 ml/½ pint milk
150 ml/¼ pint dry white wine
FOR THE GARNISH
dill sprigs
lemon twists

Put the fillets on a board, skinned side uppermost. Mix together the breadcrumbs, lemon rind and juice, dill, cream cheese, salt and pepper. Mix in enough egg to make a soft consistency. Place a spoonful of the stuffing on to each fillet and roll up. Place in an ovenproof dish and cover with greased foil. Bake in a moderate oven for 20-25 minutes.

To make the sauce, melt the butter or margarine over a gentle heat, add the flour, then gradually add the milk and wine and bring the sauce to the boil, stirring continuously. Reduce the heat and simmer gently for 2 minutes. Season to taste and pour over the stuffed plaice fillets. Garnish with fresh dill and lemon twists and serve immediately.

48 BAKED STUFFED TROUT

Preparation time:
10 minutes

Cooking time:
20-25 minutes

Oven temperature:
200 C, 400 F, gas 6

Serves 4

Calories:
445 per portion

YOU WILL NEED:
1 onion, finely chopped
25 g/1 oz butter or margarine
100 g/4 oz frozen chopped spinach
100 g/4 oz fresh brown breadcrumbs
50 g/2 oz flaked almonds, roughly
    chopped
grated rind of 1 lemon
¼ teaspoon grated nutmeg
salt and pepper
1 egg, lightly beaten
4 medium trout, cleaned, washed and
    dried
2 tablespoons olive oil
FOR THE GARNISH
lime twists
dill sprigs

Cook the onion in the butter or margarine until soft. Cover the spinach with boiling water, boil for 2 minutes, drain and squeeze dry. Mix together the onion, spinach, breadcrumbs, almonds, grated lemon rind, nutmeg and seasoning. Combine this stuffing with the egg. Divide into four and use to fill the cavity in each fish.

Place the fish in a shallow ovenproof dish, brush with the oil and bake in a moderately hot oven for 20-25 minutes or until the flesh flakes easily. Serve immediately, garnished with lime twists and fresh dill.

■ COOK'S TIP

To make lemon twists, thinly slice a lemon and cut a slit in to the centre of each slice. Twist the slices from the cuts.

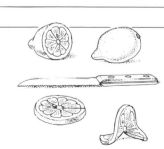

■ FREEZER TIP

To freeze whole fish, like mackerel or trout, stuff the body cavity with a small roll of foil so that the fish stays a good shape.

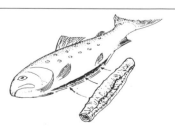

49 TROUT WITH ALMONDS

Preparation time:
10 minutes

Cooking time:
10 minutes

Serves 4

Calories:
445 per portion

YOU WILL NEED:
salt and pepper
25 g/1 oz plain flour
4 medium trout, cleaned, washed and
    dried
100 g/4 oz butter or margarine
50 g/2 oz flaked almonds
2 tablespoons lemon juice
2 tablespoons chopped parsley
FOR THE GARNISH
lemon wedges
parsley sprigs

Add the seasoning to the flour and coat the trout with the flour.

Melt half the butter or margarine in a large frying pan and fry two trout gently over a medium heat for 4-5 minutes on each side, or until golden. Drain the fish and transfer to a serving dish to keep warm. Fry the remaining trout in the same way.

When the fish are cooked, add the remaining butter to the frying pan and return it to the heat. When the fat is hot, fry the almonds until golden, quickly add the lemon juice, chopped parsley, and seasoning to taste. Stir well.

Pour the sauce over the trout, garnish with lemon wedges and parsley sprigs. Serve immediately with Duchesse Potatoes (see recipe 106) and a green vegetable.

■ MICROWAVE TIP

*Cook trout with 25 g/1 oz
butter in a covered dish 12
minutes on full power.
Brown 50 g/2 oz flaked
almonds with 25 g/1 oz
butter in a mug 4 minutes.*

50 PIQUANT MACKEREL

Preparation time:
20 minutes

Cooking time:
25 minutes

Serves 4

Calories:
390 per portion

YOU WILL NEED:
4 mackerel, halved and filleted
1 tablespoon oil
salt and pepper
juice of 1 lemon
25 g/1 oz butter or margarine
25 g/1 oz plain flour
300 ml/½ pint milk
2 teaspoons mustard powder
1 teaspoon white wine vinegar
1 teaspoon honey
1 tablespoon chopped parsley
FOR THE GARNISH
sprigs of flat-leaved parsley
lemon and lime slices

Place the mackerel fillets on a sheet of greased foil and brush with the oil. Season generously with salt and pepper, sprinkle over the lemon juice. Fold the fillets into little parcels, wrap them securely in the foil. Cook in a steamer for 20-25 minutes. Meanwhile, melt the butter or margarine over a gentle heat, add the flour, then gradually add the milk, stirring continuously. Bring the sauce to the boil, reduce the heat, add the remaining ingredients, season to taste and simmer for 2 minutes.

Unwrap the fish and transfer to a serving dish, reserving the cooking liquor. Keep the fish warm. Add the cooking liquor to the sauce and simmer for a further few minutes, then pour over the mackerel. Garnish with parsley sprigs and halved slices of lemon and lime.

■ COOK'S TIP

*A good lemon squeezer is a
useful kitchen utensil.
Decide which type you
prefer and invest in a sturdy
one.*

51 HERRINGS WITH SOURED CREAM SAUCE

Preparation time:
15 minutes

Cooking time:
12 minutes

Serves 4

Calories:
435 per portion

YOU WILL NEED:
4 fresh herrings
1 tablespoon oil
1 tablespoon white wine vinegar
salt and pepper
4 spring onions, chopped
300 ml/½ pint soured cream
1 teaspoon mustard powder
cayenne
1 tablespoon chopped fresh dill
FOR THE GARNISH
cayenne
halved lemon slices
1 teaspoon chopped fresh dill, plus a
    few sprigs

Scale and gut the herrings. Wash the insides and outsides of the fish and pat dry. Cut slits down both sides of each fish. Brush the fish with oil, then spoon the vinegar into the slits and season the fish generously.

Heat the grill to medium heat and grill the herrings on one side for 6 minutes. Turn the fish over, brush with a little more oil and cook for a further 6 minutes. Transfer the herrings to a serving plate and keep warm.

Mix the remaining ingredients together. Pour the sauce into a small serving bowl, and sprinkle with cayenne and dill. Garnish the fish with halved lemon slices and sprigs of dill and serve with the sauce.

52 SALMON MOUSSE

Preparation time:
15 minutes, plus 1 hour to chill

Serves 4

Calories:
365 per portion

YOU WILL NEED:
1 tablespoon gelatine
2 tablespoons hot water
1 × 213 g/7½ oz can salmon
150 ml/¼ pint natural yogurt
150 ml/¼ pint mayonnaise
1 tablespoon tomato ketchup
salt and pepper
2 egg whites
FOR THE GARNISH
orange slices
lime slices
parsley sprigs
dill sprigs

Sprinkle the gelatine on to the hot water in a bowl. Stand the bowl over a saucepan of simmering water and stir until dissolved.

Flake the salmon into a bowl, remove any remaining bones, and add the natural yogurt. Stir in the mayonnaise, then the tomato ketchup, gelatine and seasoning. Whisk the egg whites until stiff but not dry and fold into the salmon mixture. Pour the mixture into a serving bowl and chill for an hour or until set.

Garnish the mousse with orange and lime slices, dill and parsley sprigs and serve with triangles of toast and a salad.

COOK'S TIP

To make your own soured cream, add 1-2 tablespoons lemon juice to 150 ml/¼ pint single cream

COOK'S TIP

The mousse can be set in a fish-shaped mould for elegant presentation. Serve turned out on a flat serving platter.

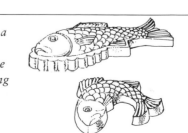

53 FISH RAGOUT

Preparation time:
15 minutes

Cooking time:
20-25 minutes

Oven temperature:
200 C, 400 F, gas 6

Serves 4

Calories:
180 per portion

YOU WILL NEED:
450 g/1 lb cod, coley or haddock
    fillets, skinned
1 onion, sliced into rings
1 garlic clove, crushed
1 green pepper, seeded and sliced into
    rings
100 g/4 oz button mushrooms
1-2 tablespoons oil
1 × 400 g/14 oz can of chopped
    tomatoes
150 ml/¼ pint dry white wine
½ teaspoon chopped fresh basil
salt and pepper
FOR THE GARNISH
fresh basil leaves
1 tablespoon chopped parsley

Rinse the fish, cut it into cubes, then put into an ovenproof dish. Fry the onion, garlic, pepper and mushrooms in the oil for 2-3 minutes, then add to the fish. Mix together the tomatoes, wine, basil, salt and pepper. Pour over the fish mixture. Cover the dish with foil and bake in a moderately hot oven for 20-25 minutes.

Serve immediately with parslied boiled rice, garnishing with fresh basil leaves and chopped parsley.

54 FISH CAKES

Preparation time:
20 minutes

Cooking time:
20 minutes

Serves 4

Calories:
390 per portion

YOU WILL NEED:
225 g/8 oz coley, cubed
knob of butter
salt and pepper
225 g/8 oz mashed potatoes
100 g/4 oz Cheddar cheese, grated
25 g/1 oz plain flour
1 egg, lightly beaten
100 g/4 oz fresh white breadcrumbs
oil for frying
FOR THE GARNISH
lemon slices
lime slices
parsley sprigs

Place the fish on a buttered flameproof plate, season and cover with foil. Steam over a pan of boiling water for 10-15 minutes or until the fish flakes easily.

Flake the fish and mix with the potato and cheese. Season, divide the mixture into eight portions and pat each into a round cake. Coat the fish cakes in the flour, dip into the egg and then into the breadcrumbs. Heat the oil in a frying pan and fry the fish cakes until golden brown on the underside, then turn and cook until golden on the other side. Drain on absorbent kitchen paper.

Garnish the fish cakes with lemon and lime slices and parsley sprigs.

■ COOK'S TIP

*Fresh basil tastes
significantly superior to its
dried counterpart. Grow
your own in a pot indoors,
positioned on a light
windowsill.*

■ FREEZER TIP

*Freeze the cakes before
frying – put them on a
baking tray covered with
cling film and open freeze.
Pack in freezer bags
when hard.*

55 FISHERMAN'S PIE

Preparation time:
20 minutes

Cooking time:
35 minutes

Oven temperature:
200 C, 400 F, gas 6

Serves 4

Calories:
760 per portion

YOU WILL NEED:
450 g/1 lb cod or coley, cubed
knob of butter
salt and pepper
1 teaspoon lemon juice
1 × recipe white sauce (recipe 156)
1 × 198 g/7 oz can sweetcorn, drained
175 g/6 oz Cheddar cheese, grated
1 tablespoon chopped parsley
pinch of mustard powder
4 hard-boiled eggs, roughly chopped
450 g/1 lb mashed potato with a little
    milk, butter and seasoning added

Place the fish on a buttered flameproof plate and season with salt, pepper and lemon juice. Cover the plate with foil or another plate and steam over a pan of boiling water for 10-15 minutes or until the fish flakes easily. Strain any juices and reserve for the sauce.

Bring the sauce to the boil, add the reserved fish stock and the sweetcorn, reduce the heat and simmer for 2 minutes, stirring occasionally. Remove the pan from the heat, blend in the cheese, parsley, salt, pepper and mustard. Finally add the eggs and the flaked fish. Pour into an ovenproof dish. Spread or pipe the prepared potato over the fish and bake in a moderately hot oven for 20 minutes or until the top is golden.

56 CRISPY FISH STICKS

Preparation time:
20 minutes

Cooking time:
5-10 minutes

Serves 4

Calories:
355 per portion

YOU WILL NEED:
8 whiting fillets
25 g/1 oz plain flour
salt and pepper
1 egg, beaten
100 g/4 oz sage and onion stuffing mix
2-4 tablespoons oil
FOR THE SAUCE
150 ml/¼ pint thick-set natural yogurt
50 g/2 oz cucumber, diced
1 tablespoon wholegrain mustard
salt
cayenne
FOR THE GARNISH
lime twists
dill sprigs

Skin the whiting fillets and cut the flesh into fine strips. Mix the flour with the seasoning and use to coat the fish strips. Dip each fish strip into the beaten egg and then into the stuffing mix, pressing it on well. Heat the oil in a frying pan, add the fish strips and fry them, turning once or twice, until golden and crisp. Drain on absorbent kitchen paper, transfer to a serving dish and keep warm.

To make the sauce, mix all the ingredients together, seasoning to taste, and pour into a small serving bowl. Serve as an accompaniment to the fish sticks. Garnish the fish sticks with lime twists and dill sprigs.

■ MICROWAVE TIP

Instead of steaming the fish over a saucepan of water, put it in a shallow microwave-proof dish with 2-3 tablespoons hot water. Cover with microwave cling film and cook on full power for about 15 minutes, or until the fish is only just cooked.

■ COOK'S TIP

To dice cucumber, cut into 3-4 slices lengthways. Put these cut side down and cut into fairly thin strips lengthways, then across.

57 FISH BALLS

Preparation time:
10 minutes

Cooking time:
10 minutes

Serves 4

Calories:
245 per portion

YOU WILL NEED:

450 g/1 lb white fish, for example,
    hake, whiting, or cod
50 g/2 oz fresh white breadcrumbs
25 g/1 oz sesame seeds
1 egg, lightly beaten
1 teaspoon Worcestershire sauce
1 tablespoon soy sauce
2 tablespoons tomato ketchup
1 tablespoon chopped parsley
salt and pepper
oil for frying
FOR THE GARNISH
tomato rose
parsley sprig

Skin the fish and chop the flesh, removing any bones. Mix the chopped fish with the remaining ingredients. Take small spoonfuls of the fish mixture and roll into balls the size of marbles.

Heat the oil in a saucepan and fry the fish balls a few at a time for 3-4 minutes or until golden. Drain on absorbent kitchen paper and keep warm until all the fish balls are cooked.

Serve hot with boiled rice and stir-fried vegetables, garnishing with a tomato rose and parsley sprig.

58 SEAFOOD CURRY

Preparation time:
20 minutes

Cooking time:
25-30 minutes

Serves 4

Calories:
260 per portion

YOU WILL NEED:

450 g/1 lb white fish fillets, for
    example, haddock, coley
    or whiting, skinned
1-2 tablespoons oil
2 onions, finely chopped
2 garlic cloves, crushed
1 green pepper, seeded and diced
2 tablespoons curry powder
2 teaspoons chilli powder
25 g/1 oz plain flour
600 ml/1 pint hot water
100 g/4 oz cooked mussels
100 g/4 oz peeled cooked prawns
4 tomatoes, peeled, seeded and
    quartered
salt and pepper
FOR THE GARNISH
whole prawns
coriander sprigs

Cut the fish into cubes. Heat the oil in a frying pan, add the onions, garlic and pepper and fry until softened, but not browned. Add the spices and flour and cook gently. Gradually add the water, stirring all the time. Bring the mixture to the boil, reduce the heat and simmer gently, then add the white fish and cook for 15 minutes. Add the mussels, prawns and tomatoes, season to taste and cook for a further 5-10 minutes.

Garnish with whole prawns and coriander sprigs and serve at once with boiled rice and poppadums.

■ COOK'S TIP

To prevent this fish mixture sticking to your hands as you shape it, dampen your hands with cold water. If the mixture begins to stick, dampen your hands again.

■ COOK'S TIP

If you cook poppadums in a frying pan, use two fish slices to prevent them from curling up as they cook.

59 KIPPERS WITH LEMON BUTTER

Preparation time:	YOU WILL NEED:
0 minutes	8 kipper fillets
	1 small onion, thinly sliced
Cooking time:	75 g/3 oz butter
5-8 minutes	grated rind and juice of ½ lemon
	1 tablespoon chopped parsley
Serves 4	salt and pepper
	FOR THE GARNISH
Calories:	lemon twists
575 per portion	parsley sprigs

Skin the kippers and remove any obvious bones. Brush a grill grid with oil, place the kippers on top and arrange the onion rings on top.

Beat the butter until pale and creamy, then gradually work the rind and juice of the lemon into the butter. Beat in the parsley and seasoning. Dot the lemon butter over the fish.

Grill the kippers for 5-8 minutes. Garnish with lemon twists and parsley sprigs, and serve with a fresh green salad and wholemeal bread.

60 QUICK TUNA BAKE

Preparation time:	YOU WILL NEED:
10 minutes	2 × 198 g/7 oz cans tuna, drained
	4 spring onions, chopped
Cooking time:	1 × 425 g/15 oz can mushroom soup
20-25 minutes	100 g/4 oz Cheddar cheese, grated
Oven temperature:	1 teaspoon chopped fresh dill
200 C, 400 F, gas 6	¼ teaspoon Worcestershire sauce
	salt and pepper
Serves 4	225 g/8 oz fresh brown breadcrumbs
Calories:	knob of butter
480 per portion	dill sprig, to garnish

Flake the tuna and mix together with the onion, soup, cheese, dill, Worcestershire sauce, salt and pepper.

Pour some of the fish sauce into an ovenproof dish. Add a layer of breadcrumbs, followed by a layer of sauce. Continue layering in this fashion until all the ingredients have been used up. Finish with a layer of breadcrumbs on the top, dot the surface with the butter and bake in a moderately hot oven for 20-25 minutes. Serve immediately, garnished with a sprig of dill and accompanied by a green salad.

COOK'S TIP

To make an interesting, crunchy green salad, include some bean sprouts, fine strips of celery and sliced avocado with more traditional ingredients.

COOK'S TIP

A quick way of 'chopping' spring onions: wash and trim them, then hold them over a bowl and snip them up from green end toward the root.

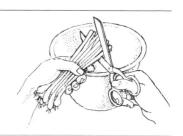

CASSEROLES & STEWS

When casseroling or stewing, the cheaper cuts of meat are used as this moist cooking method tenderises and extracts the flavour. The addition of vegetables makes many of these recipes all-in-one dishes. Most of the recipes in this chapter are suitable for freezing and reheating in a micro-wave. Some will need a topping added after reheating.

61 BEEF IN BEER

Preparation time:
20 minutes

Cooking time:
1 hour 45 minutes

Oven temperature:
160 C, 325 F, gas 3

Serves 4

Calories:
525 per portion

YOU WILL NEED:
8 button onions
100 g/4 oz carrots
2 celery sticks, cut in chunks
1 green pepper, seeded and sliced into
    rings
100 g/4 oz button mushrooms
2 tablespoons oil
575 g/1¼ lb lean braising steak, cut
    into cubes
40 g/1½ oz plain flour
¼ teaspoon mustard powder
salt and pepper
300 ml/½ pint beer
300 ml/½ pint beef stock
100 g/4 oz rindless streaky bacon
1 bay leaf
FOR THE GARNISH
1 tablespoon chopped parsley
bay leaves

Cook the vegetables in the oil for 5 minutes, then transfer to a casserole, reserving the oil. Coat the meat cubes in a mixture of the flour, mustard and seasoning. Fry a few pieces at a time in the reserved oil until just starting to brown. Add to the casserole. Stir any remaining flour into the fat in the pan. Gradually add the beer and stock and bring to the boil. Pour into the casserole. Cut the bacon rashers in half, roll up each half rasher and add to the casserole. Add the bay leaf and stir well. Cover the casserole and cook in a moderate oven for 1½ hours or until the meat is tender. Garnish as shown and serve.

▇ COOK'S TIP

To coat meat cubes, or similar items in flour, put the flour in a polythene bag. Add the meat and, holding the end of the bag firmly closed, shake well.

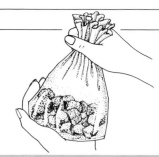

62 BOEUF BOURGUIGNONNE

Preparation time:
20 minutes

Cooking time:
1 hour 45 minutes

Oven temperature:
180 C, 350 F, gas 4

Serves 4

Calories:
515 per portion

YOU WILL NEED:
575 g/1¼ lb chuck steak, cut into cubes
25 g/1 oz plain flour
2-3 tablespoons oil
100 g/4 oz rindless streaky bacon, diced
1 onion, sliced
1 garlic clove, crushed
100 g/4 oz mushrooms, sliced
300 ml/½ pint dry red wine
600 ml/1 pint beef stock
bouquet garni
salt and pepper
1 tablespoon chopped parsley, to
    garnish

Coat the meat cubes in the flour. Heat the oil in a frying pan, brown the meat and transfer to a casserole.

Cook the diced bacon in the oil, until golden in colour and add to the meat. Gently cook the onion and garlic in the frying pan until soft, add the mushrooms and continue cooking for 2-3 minutes. Put all the vegetables in the casserole and pour in the red wine and beef stock. Add the bouquet garni and seasoning and stir well. Cover the casserole and cook in a moderate oven for 1½ hours or until the meat is tender.

Serve with parslied boiled rice and a green salad. Garnish with chopped parsley, and any fresh herbs.

▇ COOK'S TIP

To crush garlic, without a crusher, sprinkle a peeled clove with a little salt. Crush with the flat, wide blade of a knife, pressing with the palm of your hand.

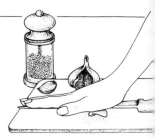

63 BEEF COBBLER

Preparation time: 20 minutes	**YOU WILL NEED:** 575 g/1¼ lb stewing or braising steak, cut into cubes
Cooking time: 2 hours 25 minutes	25 g/1 oz plain flour 1 teaspoon dried mixed herbs
Oven temperature: 160 C, 325 F, gas 3 and 220 C, 425 F, gas 7	salt and pepper 1 onion, chopped 3 tablespoons oil 100 g/4 oz baby carrots
Serves 4	2 parsnips, quartered and sliced 600 ml/1 pint beef stock
Calories: 750 per portion	100 g/4 oz frozen peas FOR THE TOPPING 225 g/8 oz self-raising flour 50 g/2 oz butter or margarine 1 egg, beaten plus extra to glaze 3 tablespoons milk

Toss the meat in the flour, herbs and seasoning. Cook in the oil until browned. Transfer to a casserole. Cook the onion in the oil until soft and add to the casserole with the carrots, parsnips and beef stock. Season to taste. Cover and cook in a moderate oven for about 2 hours. Stir in the peas.

Sift the flour and a pinch of salt into a bowl, rub in the fat until the mixture resembles fine breadcrumbs. Stir in the beaten egg and enough milk to make a soft dough. Roll out on a lightly floured work surface to about 2.5 cm/1 inch thick. Cut into rounds using a 5 cm/2 inch scone cutter. Place the cobblers on top of the meat in the casserole, increase the oven heat and bake for 15 minutes.

64 LANCASHIRE HOT POT

Preparation time: 10 minutes	**YOU WILL NEED:** 675-1 kg/1½-2¼ lb middle or best end neck of lamb
Cooking time: 2 hours	4 lambs' kidneys, skinned and cored 2 carrots, sliced
Oven temperature: 160 C, 325 F, gas 3 and 200 C, 400 F, gas 6	1 small turnip, diced 2 onions, chopped salt and pepper 450 g/1 lb potatoes, sliced
Serves 4	300 ml/½ pint lamb or beef stock 25 g/1 oz butter or margarine
Calories: 705 per portion	1 teaspoon chopped parsley, to garnish

Cut the lamb and the kidneys into neat pieces and place in alternate layers with the carrot, turnip and onion in a casserole. Season with salt and pepper.

Finish the hot pot with layers of sliced potatoes. Pour over the stock and dot the top with small pieces of butter or margarine. Cover the casserole with a lid and place in a moderate oven for about 2 hours until the meat is cooked. Uncover the casserole for the last 30 minutes and increase the oven temperature to moderately hot to brown the top layer of potatoes.

Serve immediately garnished with chopped parsley.

◼ FREEZER TIP

To freeze the cooked cobbler, first line the casserole with double-thick foil, allowing plenty of overlap round the rim. Cook the casserole and cobbler in the lined dish, then cool and lightly cover. Freeze. The cobbler can then be removed from the dish, packed in extra foil, and stored.

◼ COOK'S TIP

To core kidneys, cut them in half, then use kitchen scissors to snip out the white cores.

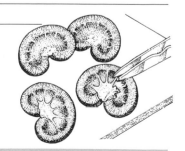

65 IRISH STEW

Preparation time:
20 minutes

Cooking time:
2 hours

Serves 4

Calories:
685 per portion

YOU WILL NEED:
2 tablespoons oil
450 g/1 lb potatoes, thinly sliced
675-1kg/1½-2¼ lb middle or scrag end
  neck of lamb or mutton
3 onions, thinly sliced
salt and pepper
900 ml/1½ pints lamb stock
chopped parsley, to garnish

Heat the oil in a large saucepan and brown the sliced potatoes. Remove the potates and reserve. Cut the lamb or mutton into neat joints, then layer the lamb, onion and potato in the saucepan, seasoning each layer well. Pour over the stock and bring the stew slowly to the boil. Reduce the heat, cover with a lid and simmer gently for 2 hours or until the meat is cooked.

Garnish the stew with parsley and serve with seasonal vegetables.

66 HUNGARIAN GOULASH

Preparation time:
15 minutes

Cooking time:
2½-3 hours

Oven temperature:
160 C, 325 F, gas 3

Serves 4

Calories:
495 per portion

YOU WILL NEED:
25 g/1 oz plain flour
¼ teaspoon mustard powder
1 tablespoon paprika
salt and pepper
575 g/1¼ lb stewing or braising steak,
  cut into cubes
3 tablespoons oil
2 onions, sliced into rings
1 red pepper, seeded and sliced
1 green pepper, seeded and sliced
450 g/1 lb tomatoes, peeled and
  quartered
600 ml/1 pint beef stock
150 ml/¼ pint soured cream
1 tablespoon chopped parsley, to
  garnish

Mix together the flour, mustard, paprika, salt and pepper and toss the meat cubes in the mixture. Heat the oil in a frying pan and cook the cubes of meat until brown on all sides. Transfer to a casserole. Gently fry the onions and peppers in the remaining fat until soft, and add to the casserole with the tomatoes and beef stock.

Mix the ingredients together well. Cover the casserole with a lid and cook in a moderate oven for 2-2½ hours or until the meat is tender.

Pour the soured cream over the meat and serve immediately, garnished with chopped parsley,

---

■ COOK'S TIP

Trim excess fat from lamb before casseroling. If the casserole looks greasy, leave to stand for 5 minutes, then use a large spoon to skim off the fat.

■ MICROWAVE TIP

Use rump steak, cut across the grain into small slices. Flour the meat, then mix in all ingredients. Microwave on full power for 20 minutes.

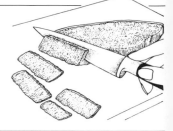

67 CASSOULET

Preparation time:
10 minutes, plus
overnight soaking

Cooking time:
2½ hours

Oven temperature:
160 C, 325 F, gas 3

Serves 4

Calories:
605 per portion

YOU WILL NEED:
350 g/12 oz haricot beans
2 onions, chopped
100 g/4 oz rindless streaky bacon,
    chopped
100 g/4 oz cervelat sausage, sliced
4 chicken drumsticks
225 g/8 oz tomatoes, peeled and
    quartered
3 tablespoons tomato purée
900 ml/1½ pints chicken stock
bouquet garni
salt and pepper
1 teaspoon chopped parsley, to
    garnish

Soak the haricot beans in cold water overnight, then drain well. Mix the beans, onion, bacon, sausage, chicken and tomatoes in a casserole. Add the tomato purée, chicken stock, bouquet garni, season well and mix together.

Cover the casserole with a lid and cook in a moderate oven for about 2½ hours until the haricot beans are cooked.

Serve immediately, garnished with chopped parsley.

68 SWEET 'N' SOUR PORK CASSEROLE

Preparation time:
20 minutes

Cooking time:
1 hour 45 minutes

Oven temperature:
160 C, 325 F, gas 3

Serves 4

Calories:
435 per portion

YOU WILL NEED:
25 g/1 oz plain flour
1 teaspoon ground ginger
salt and pepper
575 g/1¼ lb lean pork, cut into
    2.5 cm/1 inch cubes
1 onion, finely chopped
1 green pepper, seeded and sliced
2 tablespoons oil
150 ml/¼ pint chicken stock
1 × 454 g/1 lb can pineapple chunks
2 tablespoons soy sauce
3 tablespoons vinegar
50 g/2 oz no-need-to-soak dried
    apricots
FOR THE GARNISH
tomato rose
cucumber leaves

Mix the flour, ground ginger, salt and pepper together and toss the pork in the mixture. Fry the onion and pepper in the oil for 2-3 minutes. Transfer to a casserole.

Brown the pork cubes in the oil, then add to the casserole. Stir any remaining flour into the pan, blend in the stock and the juice from the pineapple. Bring to the boil, then add to the casserole with the remaining ingredients. Cover and cook in a moderate oven for 1½ hours. Serve with boiled rice, garnished as shown.

■ COOK'S TIP

Cervelat is a smoked, moist sausage, usually containing finely minced beef and pork. It is made in various European countries. Cervelat is matured for a shorter time than the Italian salami sausage, and as a result is more pliable. It is also less highly seasoned. Select from a delicatessen.

■ FREEZER TIP

Lean pork microwaves well. Mix all the ingredients, coating meat in flour and omitting oil. Microwave on full power for 15-20 minutes.

69   PORK AND DUMPLINGS

Preparation time:
20 minutes

Cooking time:
2 hours 45 minutes

Oven temperature:
180 C, 350 F, gas 4

Serves 4

Calories:
570 per portion

YOU WILL NEED:
575 g/1¼ lb lean boneless pork, cut
   into cubes
25 g/1 oz butter or margarine
2 onions, chopped
100 g/4 oz no-need-to-soak dried
   apricots
25 g/1 oz plain flour
600 ml/1 pint chicken stock
300 ml/½ pint dry cider
salt and pepper
100 g/4 oz self-raising flour
1 tablespoon chopped parsley
50 g/2 oz suet
2 tablespoons water
FOR THE GARNISH
halved orange slices
rosemary sprigs

Cook the pork cubes in the butter or margarine until golden, then transfer to a casserole. Cook the onion in the remaining fat until soft and add to the casserole with the cider. Mix all the ingredients together, season, cover, and cook in a moderate oven for 2 hours.

Sift the flour and a pinch of salt into a bowl, add the parsley and suet and mix well. Stir in the water and blend to make a soft dough. Divide and roll into small balls on a lightly floured surface. Add the dumplings to the casserole and cook for a further 30 minutes, or until the dumplings are cooked. Garnish as shown.

70   COQ AU VIN

Preparation time:
10 minutes

Cooking time:
1 hour 15 minutes

Oven temperature:
180 C, 350 F, gas 4

Serves 4

Calories:
345 per portion

YOU WILL NEED:
2 garlic cloves, crushed
½ teaspoon salt
4 chicken joints
25 g/1 oz butter or margarine
2 tablespoons oil
12 button onions
100 g/4 oz button mushrooms
25 g/1 oz plain flour
300 ml/½ pint dry red wine
150 ml/¼ pint chicken stock
bouquet garni
1 teaspoon brown sugar
salt and pepper
chopped parsley, to garnish

Rub the crushed garlic and salt into each chicken joint. Heat the butter or margarine and oil in a frying pan and cook the chicken joints until golden on all sides. Transfer the joints to a casserole.

Fry the onions and mushrooms in the remaining fat until golden and add to the casserole.

Stir the flour into the pan, add the wine and bring to the boil. Pour over the chicken joints. Add the stock, bouquet garni and sugar to the casserole, then season well. Cover the casserole with a lid or foil and cook in a moderate oven for about 1 hour. Remove the bouquet garni.

Serve garnished with chopped parsley.

■ COOK'S TIP

A flameproof casserole is useful for this type of dish. The ingredients can be browned and casseroled in the one pan.

■ COOK'S TIP

For an excellent flavour, marinate the chicken joints in the wine overnight. Drain, reserving the wine and cook as above.

71 TURKEY WITH PEACHES

Preparation time:
15 minutes

Cooking time:
30 minutes

Serves 4

Calories:
315 per portion

YOU WILL NEED:
25 g/1 oz plain flour
½ teaspoon grated nutmeg
salt and pepper
4 turkey fillets, cut into fine strips
2 tablespoons oil
1 onion, thinly sliced
1 × 227 g/8 oz can peach slices,
    drained
300 ml/½ pint chicken or turkey stock
150 ml/¼ pint soured cream
FOR THE GARNISH
chopped parsley
peach slices
bay leaves

Mix together the flour, nutmeg, salt and pepper and toss the turkey strips in the seasoned flour. Heat the oil in a frying pan and brown the turkey strips all over. Add the onion and cook for a further 2-3 minutes until soft. Add the peach slices, reserving a few for garnish, and chicken stock to the pan and bring to the boil. Reduce the heat and simmer gently for 20 minutes.

Remove the pan from the heat and add the soured cream. Reheat without boiling. Garnish with chopped parsley, reserved peach slices and bay leaves, and serve with a mixed salad.

72 CHICKEN FRICASSEE

Preparation time:
15 minutes

Cooking time:
30 minutes

Serves 4

Calories:
335 per portion

YOU WILL NEED:
4 boneless breasts of chicken, cut into
    1-cm/½-in wide strips
25 g/1 oz plain flour
50 g/2 oz butter or margarine
1 onion, chopped
100 g/4 oz mushrooms, sliced
½ teaspoon dried thyme
salt and pepper
150 ml/¼ pint chicken stock
150 ml/¼ pint dry white wine
150 ml/¼ pint soured cream
zested lemon rind, to garnish

Toss the chicken strips in the flour. Heat the butter or margarine in a frying pan and cook the chopped onion until soft. Add the mushrooms and cook for another 2 minutes. Add the chicken strips and cook until they are golden all over. Sprinkle over the thyme, and season to taste.

Mix in the stock and wine and bring to the boil, then reduce the heat and simmer gently for 20 minutes. Reduce the heat further, stir in the soured cream and cook until the sauce is warmed through, but do not allow the sauce to boil.

Garnish with lemon rind and serve the chicken with parslied boiled rice and buttered carrots.

■ COOK'S TIP

*Serve fresh spinach noodles
with this dish. Cook fresh
pasta in boiling salted water
for about 5 minutes. Drain,
butter and serve.*

■ COOK'S TIP

*If your eyes run very badly
when peeling onions, then
hold the onions under a
slow running cold tap.*

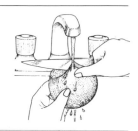

73 CHICKEN CURRY

Preparation time:
20 minutes

Cooking time:
50 minutes

Serves 4

Calories:
480 per portion

YOU WILL NEED:
3 tablespoons oil
575 g/1¼ lb boneless chicken breast,
cut into cubes
2 onions, chopped
2 garlic cloves, crushed
1 green pepper, seeded and chopped
2 tablespoons garam masala
1-2 teaspoons chilli powder
25 g/1 oz plain flour
50 g/2 oz desiccated coconut
50 g/2 oz ground almonds
450 ml/¾ pint chicken stock
450 g/1 lb tomatoes, peeled and
quartered
2 tablespoons lemon juice
salt and pepper
chopped fresh coriander, to garnish

Heat the oil in a large frying pan and brown the chicken cubes on all sides. Remove from the pan. Cook the onion, garlic and pepper in the oil until soft. Stir in the garam masala, chilli powder and flour and cook gently for 5 minutes. Add the coconut, almonds, chicken stock and tomatoes. Bring the mixture to the boil, reduce the heat and simmer gently for 20 minutes.

Add the chicken and lemon juice to the pan, season to taste and continue cooking for a further 20 minutes.

Garnish the curry with coriander and serve with rice and a tomato and onion salad.

■ COOK'S TIP

Coriander leaves look similar to flat-leaved parsley, but taste very different. When buying, look for roots which are left on coriander, not on parsley.

74 RABBIT CASSEROLE

Preparation time:
20 minutes, plus 2-3
hours to marinate

Cooking time:
3 hours

Oven temperature:
160 C, 325 F, gas 3

Serves 4

Calories:
340 per portion

YOU WILL NEED:
4 rabbit portions
300 ml/½ pint dry red wine
3 tablespoons vinegar
4 tablespoons oil
salt and pepper
1 bay leaf
25 g/1 oz plain flour
8-12 button onions
1 red pepper, seeded and sliced into
rings
100 g/4 oz baby carrots
300 ml/½ pint water
1 teaspoon wholegrain mustard
1 tablespoon redcurrant jelly
parsley sprigs, to garnish

Place the rabbit joints in a bowl. Mix together the wine, vinegar, 1 tablespoon of the oil, salt and pepper. Pour over the rabbit and add the bay leaf. Marinate the rabbit for 2-3 hours, turning occasionally. Remove the rabbit joints, drain on absorbent kitchen paper and coat with the flour.

Heat the remaining oil in a frying pan, fry the rabbit joints until just golden and transfer to a casserole. Cook the onions in the oil until golden and add to the casserole. Fry the pepper rings in the pan for a few minutes and add to the casserole with the remaining ingredients, seasoning to taste. Pour in the marinade and mix all the ingredients together well. Cover with a lid and cook in a moderate oven for 2½ hours until the rabbit is tender. Garnish with parsley sprigs.

■ COOK'S TIP

To seed a pepper, cut off the top, then use the point of the knife to cut through the pith round the inside. Core and seeds should come out as a whole.

75 KIDNEY AND SAUSAGE CASSEROLE

Preparation time:
15 minutes

Cooking time:
50 minutes

Oven temperature:
160 C, 325 F, gas 3

Serves 4

Calories:
615 per portion

YOU WILL NEED:
2 tablespoons oil
1 onion, sliced into rings
1 green pepper, seeded and sliced into
    rings
25 g/1 oz plain flour
pinch of mustard powder
salt and pepper
8 lamb's kidneys, cored and halved
450 g/1 lb cocktail sausages, or
    skinless chipolatas, cut into chunks
1 × 400 g/14 oz can chopped
    tomatoes
300 ml/½ pint beef stock
chopped parsley, to garnish

Heat the oil in a frying pan and cook the onion and pepper in
the oil for a few minutes. Transfer to a casserole. Mix together the flour, mustard, salt and pepper and toss the kidneys
and sausages in the seasoned flour.

Cook the kidneys and sausages in the remaining oil until
brown on all sides and transfer to the casserole. Mix in the
tomatoes and beef stock, cover the casserole with a lid and
cook in a moderate oven for 30-40 minutes.

Garnish with parsley and serve with boiled rice, or
mashed potato, piped and browned in the oven.

76 LIVER AND WATERCRESS

Preparation time:
15 minutes

Cooking time:
25-30 minutes

Serves 4

Calories:
400 per portion

YOU WILL NEED:
2 onions, sliced into rings
2 tablespoons oil
25 g/1 oz plain flour
pinch of mustard jpowder
salt and pepper
450 g/1 lb lamb's liver, sliced into
    strips
150 ml/¼ pint chicken stock
150 ml/¼ pint orange juice
bunch of watercress, trimmed and
    chopped
150 ml/¼ pint single cream
FOR THE GARNISH
orange slices
parsley sprigs

Cook the onion rings in the oil until soft. Remove from the
pan and set aside. Mix the flour with the mustard, salt and
pepper and toss the liver strips in it. Reserving the flour, fry
the liver in the oil for 2-3 minutes, then add to the cooked
onions. Stir the remaining flour into the oil in the pan, blend
in the chicken stock and orange juice and bring to the boil.
Reduce the heat, add the watercress, onion and liver and simmer for 15 minutes or until the liver is cooked through.

Stir in the cream and seasoning to taste and cook over a
gentle heat until the sauce is hot. Do not allow it to boil or the
cream will curdle. Serve the liver garnished with orange slices
and parsley sprigs and accompanied by Duchesse Potatoes
(see recipe 106) and green beans.

■ COOK'S TIP

Vary the flavour of plain
rice by adding a pinch of
turmeric, herbs, lemon rind
or chopped spring onions.

■ COOK'S TIP

To segment an orange, peel
and remove pith. Hold
orange over a bowl (to
catch juice) and cut in
between each membrane to
free the segments.

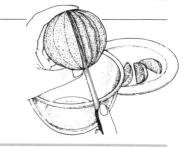

77 CHILLI CON CARNE

Preparation time:
10 minutes

Cooking time:
30-35 minutes

Serves 4

Calories:
435 per portion

YOU WILL NEED:
1 tablespoon oil
1 onion, chopped
2 garlic cloves, crushed
450 g/1 lb minced beef
15 g/½ oz plain flour
salt
2 teaspoons chilli powder
1 × 400 g/14 oz can tomatoes
300 ml/½ pint beef stock
1 × 425 g/15 oz can red kidney beans
chopped parsley, to garnish

Heat the oil in a frying pan and cook the onion and garlic until soft. Add the minced beef and cook until brown all over. Mix in the flour, salt to taste, chilli powder, tomatoes and beef stock. Stir in the mixture well and bring to the boil. Reduce the heat and simmer gently for 30 minutes, stirring occasionally.

Drain the kidney beans, add to the chilli and cook for a further 5-10 minutes or until the kidney beans are heated through.

Serve the chilli on a bed of boiled rice. Garnish with parsley.

78 MOUSSAKA

Preparation time:
30 minutes

Cooking time:
1 hour 40 minutes

Oven temperature:
180 C, 350 F, gas 4

Serves 4

Calories:
630 per portion

YOU WILL NEED:
2 aubergines, thinly sliced
salt and pepper
3 tablespoons oil
3 onions, thinly sliced
6 tomatoes, peeled
450 g/1 lb minced beef or lamb
1 tablespoon plain flour
1 tablespoon tomato purée
300 ml/½ pint beef stock
1 teaspoon dried mixed herbs
40 g/1½ oz butter or margarine
40 g/1½ oz plain flour
600 ml/1 pint milk
75 g/3 oz Cheddar cheese, grated
chopped parsley, to garnish

Sprinkle the aubergines with salt to remove bitter juices and leave covered while preparing the other vegetables. Heat the oil in a frying pan and cook the onion until soft. Remove from the pan and set aside. Slice the tomatoes. Rinse the aubergine, then dry on absorbent kitchen paper and fry in the pan, a few slices at a time, until golden on each side. Drain.

Fry the meat until browned. Stir in the flour, tomato purée, stock, herbs and seasoning. Bring to the boil, then simmer for 15 minutes. Make a cheese sauce with the remaining ingredients, as instructed in recipe 110. Layer the meat and vegetables in an ovenproof dish, then top with the cheese sauce. Bake in a moderately hot oven for 1 hour. Garnish the moussaka with chopped parsley.

■ COOK'S TIP

Dried red kidney beans need overnight soaking and rapid boiling for 3-5 minutes, then about 1 hour's simmering before use in chilli. Add extra liquid.

■ COOK'S TIP

A quick way to make cheese sauce: put all ingredients, except cheese, in a saucepan and heat slowly to boiling point, whisking continuously. Stir in cheese.

79 CHICKEN AND LEMON CASSEROLE

Preparation time:
10 minutes

Cooking time:
1 hour 15 minutes

Oven temperature:
180 C, 350 F, gas 4

Serves 4

Calories:
330 per portion

YOU WILL NEED:
4 chicken joints
salt and pepper
1 tablespoon chopped lemon thyme or thyme
grated rind and juice of 1 lemon
600 ml/1 pint chicken stock
3 teaspoons cornflour
150 ml/¼ pint double cream
FOR THE GARNISH
lemon twists
chopped lemon thyme

Place the chicken joints in a casserole, rub in a little salt and pepper and the lemon thyme or thyme. Sprinkle over the rind and juice of the lemon and the chicken stock.

Cook, covered, in a moderate oven for 1 hour. Carefully drain the liquid from the casserole into a saucepan. Return the chicken to the oven to keep warm. Mix the cornflour with a little cold water to a smooth paste, stir into the cooking liquid. Bring the liquid to the boil, stirring all the time. Reduce the heat and add the cream. Season to taste.

Pour the sauce over the joints and garnish with lemon twists and lemon thyme. Serve immediately with boiled rice and Brussels Sprouts with Chestnuts (see recipe 113).

80 SHEPHERD'S PIE

Preparation time:
20 minutes

Cooking time:
45 minutes

Oven temperature:
180 C, 350 F, gas 4

Serves 4

Calories:
525 per portion

YOU WILL NEED:
1½ tablespoons oil
1 onion, chopped
1 green pepper, seeded and chopped
450 g/1 lb minced beef
100 g/4 oz mushrooms, sliced
2 tablespoons tomato purée
1 teaspoon Worcestershire sauce
300 ml/½ pint beef stock
salt and pepper
675 g/1½ lb potatoes
25 g/1 oz butter or margarine
2-3 tablespoons milk

Heat the oil in a frying pan and cook the onion and pepper for a few minutes. Stir in the minced beef and cook until it is evenly browned. Add the mushrooms and cook until soft. Mix in the tomato purée, Worcestershire sauce, beef stock and seasoning and slowly bring the mixture to the boil. Reduce the heat and simmer gently for 20 minutes.

Meanwhile, cook the potatoes in a pan of boiling salted water for 20 minutes or until tender. Drain, mash with a fork, add the butter or margarine and the milk and beat until smooth.

Place the meat mixture in an ovenproof dish and cover with the mashed potato, forking it neatly or piping it. Bake in a moderate oven for 20 minutes or until the top is crisp and golden. Serve immediately.

■ COOK'S TIP

If you prefer, skin the chicken joints for this dish. Trim off leg and wing ends, then pull off the skin from the cut side of the joint.

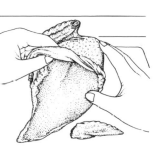

■ FREEZER TIP

Make individual pies, freeze until hard, then pack neatly in a large bag. Microwave on high for 10-20 minutes for one or two pies.

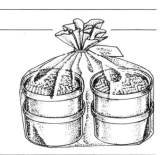

Roasts & Grills

Roasting and grilling are comparatively quick cooking methods, but only suitable for prime cuts of meat and tender poultry. There are many ways of adding flavour to the meat and in this section you will find recipes using stuffings, marinades, sauces and flavoured butters.

81 Roast chicken

Preparation time:
20 minutes

Cooking time:
see notes below

Oven temperature:
200 C, 400 F, gas 6

Serves 6

Calories:
230 per portion

YOU WILL NEED:
1 × 1.5 kg/3 lb oven-ready chicken
1-2 tablespoons oil
FOR THE STUFFING
1 tablespoon oil
1 onion, chopped
100 g/4 oz fresh white breadcrumbs
1 tablespoon dried or 3 tablespoons chopped fresh tarragon
grated rind and juice of 1 lemon
1 small egg, lightly beaten
salt and pepper
FOR THE GARNISH
lemon wedges
parsley sprigs

Weigh the chicken and calculate the cooking time. Allow 20 minutes per 450 g/1 lb plus an extra 20 minutes. Remove and reserve the giblets for gravy, then wash the chicken. Brush the chicken with the oil.

Heat the oil and cook the onion until soft. Mix with the breadcrumbs, tarragon, lemon rind and juice, egg and seasoning. Stuff the neck end of the chicken and secure with a skewer. Place the bird in a rosting tin and roast in a moderately hot oven for the calculated time.

Garnish the chicken as shown and serve with gravy (see Cook's Tip 86) and vegetables of your choice.

82 Chicken with honey

Preparation time:
10 minutes

Cooking time:
25-30 minutes

Serves 4

Calories:
320 per portion

YOU WILL NEED:
50 g/2 oz butter or margarine
2 tablespoons honey
grated rind of 1 lemon
50 g/2 oz flaked almonds
1 teaspoon wholegrain mustard
salt and pepper
4 chicken joints

Mix together the butter or margarine, honey, lemon rind, almonds, mustard and seasoning.

Spread the mixture all over the chicken joints. Cook under a moderate grill for 25-30 minutes, turning the joints once and basting occasionally.

Serve the chicken with boiled parslied rice and a crisp green salad.

■ FREEZER TIP

Fresh herbs such as tarragon freeze well. Chop finely and open freeze on a metal tray. Store in small plastic pots. Measure out from frozen.

■ MICROWAVE TIP

To measure honey easily remove lid and heat pot in the microwave for a few seconds to thin.

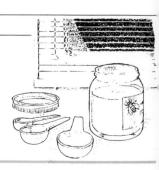

83 EASY CHICKEN KIEV

Preparation time:
20 minutes, plus 30
minutes to freeze

Cooking time:
30-40 minutes

Oven temperature:
190 C, 375 F, gas 5

Serves 4

Calories:
435 per portion

YOU WILL NEED:
4 boneless breasts of chicken
2 garlic cloves, crushed
grated rind of 1 lemon
100 g/4 oz butter
1 tablespoon chopped parsley
salt and pepper
25 g/1 oz plain flour
1 egg, lightly beaten
100 g/4 oz fresh white breadcrumbs

Beat the chicken breasts flat with a meat mallet or a rolling pin. Mix together the garlic, lemon rind, butter, parsley and seasoning to form a paste. Divide the butter evenly between the chicken breasts and carefully roll up. Secure with string.

Freeze for 15 minutes, or until the butter is firm. Coat the chicken in the flour, dip in the beaten egg and coat in the breadcrumbs, pressing firmly to make sure they stick. Return to the freezer for a further 15 minutes.

Bake the chicken Kiev in a moderately hot oven for 30-40 minutes or until the outside is golden and crisp.

Serve with boiled vegetables.

84 TANDOORI CHICKEN

Preparation time:
15 minutes, plus
overnight
marinating

Cooking time:
25-30 minutes

Serves 4

Calories:
240 per portion

YOU WILL NEED:
4 chicken joints
1 teaspoon chilli powder
1 teaspoon ground coriander
1 teaspoon ground cumin
2 teaspoons garam masala
½ teaspoon ground ginger
2 garlic cloves, crushed
juice of 1 lemon
2 tablespoons tomato purée
salt and pepper
150 ml/¼ pint natural yogurt
50 g/2 oz butter or margarine

Remove the skin from the chicken joints. Place the chicken in a glass or earthenware dish. Mix together the remaining ingredients, except for the butter or margarine. Pour the marinade over the chicken, cover and chill overnight.

Remove the chicken from the marinade and dot with the butter or margarine. Grill the chicken, turning and basting with the marinade frequently, for 25-30 minutes or until the chicken juices run clear when the joints are pierced with the point of a sharp knife.

Serve immediately with boiled rice, garnished with lemon wedges and a parsley sprig, and a mixed salad.

■ COOK'S TIP

Use a pastry brush to remove grated lemon rind from grater.

■ COOK'S TIP

Line the base of the grill pan with kitchen foil before putting the chicken on the rack for easy cleaning of grill.

85 ROAST TURKEY WITH CHESTNUT STUFFING

Preparation time:
20 minutes

Cooking time:
see notes below

Oven temperature:
220 C, 425 F, gas 7
or
160 C, 325 F, gas 3

Serves 10

Calories:
385 per portion

YOU WILL NEED:
100 g/4 oz butter or lard
1 × 3.5 kg/8 lb turkey
4 rashers rindless streaky bacon,
  chopped and fried
1 small onion, chopped
50 g/2 oz fresh white breadcrumbs
grated rind of 1 lemon
225 g/8 oz unsweetened canned
  chestnut purée
25 g/1 oz butter, melted
1 egg, lightly beaten
salt and pepper
parsley sprigs, to garnish

Spread the fat over the turkey. Combine the remaining ingredients, stuff the neck end and secure with a skewer.

Weigh the stuffed turkey and calculate the cooking time. For quick roasting method (at 220 C, 425 F, gas 7), allow 15 minutes per 450 g/1 lb, up to 5.5 kg/12 lb wieght, and 12 minutes per 450 g/1 lb over 5.5 kg/12 lb weight. For slow roasting method (at 160 C, 325 F, gas 3), allow 25 minutes per 450 g/1 lb, plus 25 minutes, up to 5.5 kg/12 lb weight and 20 minutes per 450 g/1 lb, plus 20 minutes, over 5.5 kg/12 lb weight.

Roast the turkey. Garnish with parsley and serve with thin gravy (see Cook's Tip 86), bread sauce (see Microwave Tip below), cranberry sauce, Brussels sprouts, cocktail sausages and bacon rolls.

■ MICROWAVE TIP

Bread sauce: microwave a small onion stuck with 4 cloves 1 minute. Add 300 ml/½ pint milk, cook 3 minutes. Add 50 g/2 oz breadcrumbs, cook 2 minutes. Season.

86 ROAST DUCK WITH PEAR STUFFING

Preparation time:
10 minutes

Cooking time:
2-2½ hours

Oven temperature:
190 C, 375 F, gas 5

Serves 4

Calories:
300 per portion

YOU WILL NEED:
1 × 1.75 kg/4 lb duck
salt
FOR THE STUFFING
225 g/8 oz pears, peeled, cored and
  chopped
1 onion, grated
100 g/4 oz fresh brown breadcrumbs
juice and rind of 1 lemon
2 teaspoons dried sage
salt and pepper
1 egg, lightly beaten
FOR THE GARNISH
parsley sprigs
lemon twists
chopped pears

Rinse the inside and outside of the duck and pat dry. Rub the salt over the duck. Mix the remaining ingredients together thoroughly, binding with the egg and stuff the neck end of the duck. Secure with a skewer.

Weigh the bird and calculate the cooking time. Allow 30 minutes per 450 g/1 lb. Place the duck on a wire rack in a roasting tin, prick skin with a sharp fork and roast in a moderate oven for the calculated time.

Transfer the duck to a serving plate and garnish as illustrated. Serve the duck with a thin gravy (see Cook's Tip below), roast potatoes, buttered carrots and peas.

■ COOK'S TIP

Gravy: Simmer giblets and a sliced onion in water 1 hour. Strain. Pour off fat from roasting tin, leaving about 2 tablespoons juices. Stir in 1-2 tablespoons plain flour, *depending on thickness required. Cook, stirring, 2 minutes. Blend in 450 ml/¾ pint giblet or other stock. Bring to the boil. Cook 3 minutes. Season.*

87 ROAST DUCK WITH ORANGE SAUCE

Preparation time:
20 minutes

Cooking time:
2-2½ hours

Oven temperature:
190 C, 375 F, gas 6

Serves 6

Calories:
200 per portion

YOU WILL NEED:
1 × 1.75-2.25 kg/4-5 lb duck
salt
300 ml/½ pint chicken stock
FOR THE SAUCE
1 onion, finely chopped
1 tablespoon oil
25 g/1 oz plain flour
150 ml/¼ pint orange juice
2 tablespoons brandy (optional)
salt and pepper
FOR THE GARNISH
orange slices
watercress sprigs

Weigh the duck and calculate the cooking time. Allow 30 minutes per 450 g/1 lb. Rub the salt over the duck. Place the duck on a wire rack in a roasting tin and roast in a moderately hot oven for the calculated time.

Remove the duck from the oven and place on a hot serving dish to keep warm. Pour off the fat and reserve any juices from the tin.

To make the sauce, fry the onion in the oil until soft, add the flour and gradually blend in the orange juice, stock and reserved juices. Bring the sauce to the boil, reduce the heat and simmer gently for 2 minutes, then add the brandy, if using, and seasoning.

Serve the duck garnished with orange slices and watercress sprigs and serve the sauce separately.

■ MICROWAVE TIP

Cook duck in microwave oven 25 minutes, turning dish once. Remove from dish and cook on rack in roasting tin in a very hot oven for 25 minutes.

88 ROAST BEEF

Preparation time:
5 minutes

Cooking time:
see notes below

Oven temperature:
220 C, 425 F, gas 7
or
160 C, 325 F, gas 3

Calories:
200 per 100 g/4 oz
portion lean beef

YOU WILL NEED:
1 joint of beef (see notes below)
50 g/2 oz lard or dripping, if needed
salt and pepper

Beef can be either quick roasted at a high temperature or slow roasted at a low one. Quick roasting should only be used for prime cuts of beef such as fillet, rib, topside or sirloin. Slow roasting can be used for prime cuts, aitchbone and best brisket. When quick roasting beef, allow 15 minutes per 450 g/1 lb plus 15 minutes for a rare joint, 20 minutes per 450 g/1 lb plus 20 minutes for medium rare and 25 minutes per 450 g/1 lb plus 25 minutes for a well done joint. When slow roasting beef, allow 25 minutes per 450 g/1 lb plus 25 minutes for a rare joint, 30 minutes per 450 g/1 lb plus 30 minutes for medium rare and 35 minutes per 450 g/1 lb plus 35 minutes for a well done joint. Allow 100-175 g/4-6 oz beef from a boneless joint per person and 175-225 g/6-8 oz of beef from a joint on the bone. Weigh the joint and calculate the cooking time. Spread fat over lean joints. Place the joint in a roasting tin and season. Roast for the calculated time, basting regularly.

■ COOK'S TIP

Yorkshire pudding: blend 100 g/4 oz plain flour, 1 egg and 150 ml/¼ pint milk until smooth. Stir in 150 ml/¼ pint milk and water mixed. Heat a little fat from roasting tin in 1 large tin or 12 bun tins. Pour in batter and cook in hot oven 20-40 minutes until risen and brown. For extra light and crisp puddings use 2 eggs.

89 ROAST LAMB

Preparation time:
10 minutes

Cooking time:
see notes below

Oven temperature:
190 C, 375 F, gas 5

Calories:
190 per 100 g/4 oz
portion lean roast
lamb

YOU WILL NEED:
1 leg or shoulder of lamb
salt and pepper
3 garlic cloves, thinly sliced (optional)
a few rosemary sprigs, plus extra to
*   garnish (optional)*

To roast a leg or shoulder of lamb medium rare allow 20 minutes per 450 g/1 lb, plus 20 minutes, or for a well done joint allow 25 minutes per 450 g/1 lb, plus 25 minutes. Weigh the joint and calculate the cooking time.

Rub the joint with salt and pepper, cut small incisions in the skin and insert the slices of garlic, if liked. Place the joint on a wire rack in a roasting tin in the oven. Insert a few rosemary sprigs in the joint, if liked, and roast in a moderate oven. When the lamb is cooked remove the rosemary and transfer to a hot serving dish to keep warm.

Make the gravy for lamb as described in Cook's Tip 86.

Garnish the lamb with rosemary sprigs, and serve with mint sauce, roast potatoes, carrots and a green vegetable, such as broccoli.

90 STUFFED SHOULDER OF LAMB

Preparation time:
15 minutes

Cooking time:
see notes below

Oven temperature:
190 C, 375 F, gas 5

Serves 6

Calories:
360 per 100 g/4 oz
portion lean roast
lamb with stuffing

YOU WILL NEED:
1 × 1.5-1.75 kg/3½-4 lb shoulder of
*   lamb, boned*
salt and pepper
50 g/2 oz white rice, cooked
1 small onion, finely chopped
50 g/2 oz sultanas
50 g/2 oz no-need-to-soak apricots,
*   finely chopped*
50 g/2 oz peanuts, finely chopped
1 teaspoon dried rosemary, crushed
salt and pepper
1 egg, lightly beaten
1-2 tablespoons oil

Spread out the lamb and season well with salt and pepper.

To make the stuffing, mix together the rice, onion, fruit, peanuts, rosemary and salt and pepper in a large mixing bowl. Bind well with the egg, then spread the stuffing over the lamb. Carefully roll up the lamb and secure with string. Weigh the lamb and calculate the cooking time, allowing 25 minutes per 450 g/1 lb plus an extra 25 minutes. Place the joint in a roasting tin and brush the outside with oil. Roast in a moderately hot oven for the calculated time.

Remove the string, slice and serve the lamb with gravy, baked potatoes and tomato halves filled with peas.

■ COOK'S TIP

To make mint sauce: chop 6
sprigs of mint with 1
tablespoon sugar. Place in a
bowl, add 2 tablespoons
boiling water and 4
tablespoons vinegar.

■ MICROWAVE TIP

For a 1.75 kg/4 lb joint,
cook for 30 minutes on full
power, turning 3 times.
Transfer to a conventional
oven and cook for a further
30 minutes.

91 STUFFED BREAST OF LAMB

Preparation time:
15 minutes

Cooking time:
see notes below

Oven temperature:
180 C, 350 F, gas 4

Serves 4

Calories:
450 per 100 g/4 oz
portion lean roast
lamb with stuffing

YOU WILL NEED:
1 boned breast of lamb
salt and pepper
¼ teaspoon tarragon
1 onion, grated
100 g/4 oz fresh brown breadcrumbs
100 g/4 oz dried prunes, finely
    chopped
grated rind and juice of 1 orange
grated rind of 1 lemon
50 g/2 oz blanched almonds, chopped
1 egg, lightly beaten

Spread out the breast of lamb on a board and rub in the salt, pepper and tarragon.

Mix the onion, breadcrumbs, prunes, orange rind and juice, lemon rind, almonds and salt and pepper and bind well with the egg. Spread the stuffing over the meat. Carefully roll up the lamb. Do not roll too tightly as the stuffing tends to expand slightly during cooking. Tie the joint securely with string. Weigh the stuffed lamb to calculate the cooking time. Allow 25 minutes per 450 g/1 lb plus an extra 25 minutes. Place on a wire rack in a roasting tin and cook in a moderate oven for the calculated time.

When cooked, remove the string, slice and serve with gravy (see Cook's Tip 86) and a selection of vegetables.

92 NOISETTES OF LAMB WITH SAVOURY BUTTER

Preparation time:
20 minutes, plus
30 minutes to freeze

Cooking time:
10 minutes

Serves 4

Calories:
340 per portion

YOU WILL NEED:
1 boned best end of lamb
salt and pepper
a few rosemary sprigs, plus extra to
    garnish
50 g/2 oz butter
1 garlic clove, crushed
1 tablespoon chopped parsley

Season the lamb with salt and pepper on the boned surface. Break the rosemary between your fingers and sprinkle over the lamb. Starting at one end roll up the lamb to form a Swiss roll shape. Tie the roll securely with string at 2.5 cm/1 in intervals. With a sharp knife cut the noisettes between each piece of string.

To make the savoury butter, beat the butter until pale and creamy, then work in the garlic, parsley and seasoning to taste. Turn out the butter on to a sheet of greaseproof paper and with wet hands work the butter back and forth to form a roll. Freeze for about 30 minutes.

Cook the noisettes under a hot grill for 5 minutes, then remove the pan from the heat, turn the noisettes over, add a slice of savoury butter and grill for a further 5 minutes.

Garnish the noisettes with rosemary sprigs.

■ COOK'S TIP

Blanched almonds are much easier to chop or cut into slivers if covered with boiling water for 30 seconds then drained.

■ COOK'S TIP

Flavoured butters perk up grilled meats and fish. Try anchovy butter with steak, fennel or dill butter with white fish and mustard butter with mackerel.

93 ROAST PORK

Preparation time:
15 minutes

Cooking time:
see notes below

Oven temperature:
190 C, 375 F, gas 5

Calories:
185 per 100 g/4 oz
portion lean roast
pork

YOU WILL NEED:
1 leg, loin or shoulder of pork
salt and pepper
1 tablespoon oil

The cooking time for a leg or loin of pork is 30 minutes per 450 g/1 lb plus 35 minutes, or for part of a leg or a shoulder 30 minutes per 450 g/1 lb plus 35 minutes. Weigh the joint and calculate the cooking time.

Score the rind of the joint with a sharp knife at 5-mm/¼ in intervals. Rub salt and pepper into the rind and then brush the oil over. Place the meat, rind side-up, on a wire rack standing in a roasting tin and roast in a moderate oven for the time calculated. Check the meat is cooked by inserting a skewer into the centre – the juices that emerge should be colourless.

Transfer the meat to a hot serving dish and keep warm whilst making the gravy (see Cook's Tip 86), but using half vegetable water and half cider, if liked.

Serve the pork with apple sauce and roast and boiled vegetables as accompaniments.

94 STUFFED PORK ROLL

Preparation time:
15 minutes

Cooking time:
see notes below

Oven temperature:
180 C, 350 F, gas 4

Calories:
285 per 100 g/4 oz
portion lean roast
pork with stuffing

YOU WILL NEED:
1 hand of pork, skinned and boned
salt and pepper
FOR THE STUFFING
225 g/8 oz cooking apples, peeled, cored and sliced
100 g/4 oz fresh white breadcrumbs
juice and rind of 1 lemon
½ teaspoon sage
salt and pepper
1 egg, lightly beaten

Place the pork joint on a work surface and rub in the seasoning thoroughly.

To make the stuffing, mix together the apples, breadcrumbs, lemon juice and rind, sage and seasoning. Bind the mixture together well with the egg. Spread the stuffing over the joint. Roll up and secure with string. Sprinkle salt and pepper over the top of the joint.

Weigh the pork to calculate the cooking time. Allow 30 minutes per 450 g/1 lb plus 30 minutes. Wrap the joint in foil, place in a roasting tin and bake in a moderate oven for the calculated time.

When cooked, remove the foil and string and serve sliced with gravy (see Cook's Tip 86), potato croquettes and green beans.

■ MICROWAVE TIP

To make apple sauce, put sliced apples in a large basin with sugar. Cover and cook on full power for 7 minutes. Beat well and serve in a small dish.

■ COOK'S TIP

To make breadcrumbs quickly, use a blender or food processor. Cut bread in cubes and drop into running machine through hole in lid or tube.

95 PORK CHOPS WITH ORANGE AND CASHEW NUT STUFFING

Preparation time:
15 minutes

Cooking time:
16-20 minutes

Serves 4

Calories:
370 per portion

YOU WILL NEED:
4 loin pork chops
salt and pepper
FOR THE STUFFING
1 onion, grated
grated rind of 1 orange
50 g/2 oz cashew nuts, chopped
½ teaspoon sage
1 teaspoon Dijon mustard
50 g/2 oz fresh brown breadcrumbs
salt and pepper
1 egg, lightly beaten
1-2 tablespoons oil
FOR THE GARNISH
orange slices
parsley sprigs

Cut the rind and excess fat off the chops and season the chops with salt and pepper. Carefully cut each chop horizontally, leaving joined at the bone.

Mix together the onion, orange rind, cashew nuts, sage, mustard, breadcrumbs, seasoning and bind with the egg. Place the stuffing inside the chops. Brush with the oil and cook under a medium grill for 8-10 minutes on each side or until the chops are golden and the stuffing is cooked. Serve garnished with orange slices and parsley.

96 SPICED GLAZED HAM

Preparation time:
10 minutes, plus
overnight soaking

Cooking time:
see notes below

Oven temperature:
220 C, 425 F, gas 7

Calories:
165 per 100 g/4 oz
portion lean cooked
gammon

YOU WILL NEED:
1 joint middle or corner of gammon
1.2 litres/2 pints water
1 onion
1 bay leaf
salt and pepper
100 g/4 oz soft brown sugar
grated rind of 1 orange
½ teaspoon grated nutmeg
½ teaspoon ground cinnamon
TO SERVE
3 dessert apples
cloves
zested orange rind
orange slices, to garnish

Weigh the gammon and calculate the cooking time, allowing 30 minutes per 450 g/1 lb. Soak the gammon in cold water overnight. Drain.

Put the gammon in a saucepan with the water, onion, bay leaf and seasoning. Cover, bring to the boil, then reduce the heat and simmer for 1½ hours. Drain the gammon and peel off the skin, marking the fat into diamond shapes with a sharp knife. Mix together the sugar, orange rind, nutmeg, and cinnamon for the glaze and rub into the gammon fat. Place joint in a roasting tin. Bake the gammon in a hot oven for the remainder of the calculated cooking time, or until the fat is crisp and golden. Stick the cloves in the apples and place them in the roasting tin for the final 15 minutes' cooking time, basting with any meat juices. Garnish with orange slices.

■ COOK'S TIP

For a change, substitute lemon rind and almonds for the orange rind and cashew nuts in this stuffing.

■ COOK'S TIP

For a delicious sauce with the gammon, pour a small bottle of ginger ale around the joint before roasting. If liked substitute ground ginger for the spices.

97 GAMMON STEAK WITH APRICOT AND WALNUT SAUCE

Preparation time:
15 minutes

Cooking time:
12-16 minutes

Serves 4

Calories:
330 per portion

YOU WILL NEED:
4 gammon steaks
grated rind of 1 lemon
2 tablespoons oil
salt and pepper
100 g/4 oz no-need-to-soak dried
  apricots
150 ml/¼ pint dry cider
150 ml/¼ pint water
50 g/2 oz walnuts, chopped
¼ teaspoon grated nutmeg
a little grated orange rind, to garnish

With a sharp knife trim the rind from the gammon and score the fat so that the steaks lie fat. Mix together the lemon rind, oil, salt and pepper. Brush this mixture over both sides of the gammon and cook the steaks under a hot grill for 6-8 minutes on each side.

Blend the apricots and cider in a liquidizer, then pour into a saucepan. Add the water, walnuts, nutmeg and seasoning to taste to the fruit mixture and bring the sauce to the boil. Reduce the heat and simmer gently for 5-10 minutes or until the sauce has thickened.

Arrange the gammon steaks on a serving plate, and garnish with grated orange rind. Pour over the sauce, and serve with broccoli and parslied boiled potatoes.

■ COOK'S TIP

The sauce is equally good with pork chops or roast pork. If liked, substitute 225 g/8 oz sliced apple for the apricots.

98 MEAT LOAF

Preparation time:
15 minutes

Cooking time:
1-1¼ hours

Oven temperature:
180 C, 350 F, gas 4

Serves 4

Calories:
525 per portion

YOU WILL NEED:
675 g/1½ lb minced beef
1 onion, finely chopped
1 tablespoon chopped parsley
100 g/4 oz fresh white breadcrumbs
1 egg, lightly beaten
2-3 tablespoons dry red wine
salt and pepper
1 tablespoon oil
1 onion, finely chopped
2 garlic cloves, crushed
1 × 400 g/14 oz can chopped
  tomatoes
150 ml/¼ pint beef stock
1 tablespoon chopped parsley
sliced pickled cucumber, to garnish

Grease a 1 kg/2 lb loaf tin. Mix the mince, onion, parsley, breadcrumbs, egg, red wine and seasoning together thoroughly. Pack firmly into the tin and cover with a sheet of greased foil. Bake in a moderate oven for 1-1¼ hours or until the loaf begins to shrink from the tin.

Heat the oil in a saucepan and cook the onion and garlic until soft. Blend the tomatoes in a liquidizer and add to the onion mixture with the stock, parsley and seasoning to taste. Bring the sauce to the boil, reduce the heat, and simmer for 10-15 minutes, stirring occasionally.

Tip the meat loaf out of the tin and arrange on a serving dish, then pour over the hot tomato sauce. Garnish with sliced pickled cucumber.

■ MICROWAVE TIP

Tomato sauce is easily made in the microwave. Cook onion and garlic for 4 minutes. Add remaining ingredients and cook for 7 minutes.

99 GRILLED STEAK

Preparation time:
10 minutes

Cooking time:
6-10 minutes

Serves 4

Calories:
300 per portion

YOU WILL NEED:
4 medium rump steaks
50 g/2 oz butter, melted
1 teaspoon prepared English mustard
2 garlic cloves, crushed
salt and pepper
FOR THE GARNISH
4 firm tomatoes
100 g/4 oz mushrooms
1 tablespoon chopped parsley, plus a few sprigs

Place the steaks on a rack in the grill pan. Mix together the butter, mustard, garlic and seasoning and brush half of the mixture over the steaks.

Cook under a hot grill for 1-2 minutes, then remove the pan from the heat, turn the steaks over, brush with more butter (reserving some for the garnish ingredients) and cook for a further 1-2 minutes.

Turn the grill down to a medium heat. Cut a small cross on the top of the tomatoes and arrange the tomatoes and mushrooms around the steaks. Brush the vegetables with the remaining butter. Continue cooking for 2 minutes on each side for a rare steak, 3 minutes for medium rare, and 4 minutes for well-done steak.

Transfer the steaks to a warmed serving plate and sprinkle over the chopped parsley. Add the vegetable garnishes and a few sprigs of parsley to the plate.

100 HONEY-GLAZED LAMB CHOPS

Preparation time:
10 minutes, plus 1 hour to chill

Cooking time:
10 minutes

Serves 4

Calories:
355 per portion

YOU WILL NEED:
salt and pepper
4 lamb chump chops
50 g/2 oz butter or margarine
2 tablespoons honey
2 teaspoons wholegrain mustard
FOR THE GARNISH
chopped parsley
watercress sprigs

Season the chops well and beat the butter or margarine until pale and creamy. Blend in the honey, mustard and seasoning to taste to form a smooth paste. Brush the honey mixture over the chops, cover and chill for about an hour.

Grill the chops under a hot grill for 5 minutes on each side.

Serve the chops, garnished with a little chopped parsley and sprigs of watercress and accompanied by boiled broccoli and jacket potatoes.

■ COOK'S TIP

Rump, usually the cheapest grilling steak, should have a good layer of fat along the edge. Sirloin is dearer and leaner. Fillet steak is very lean but expensive.

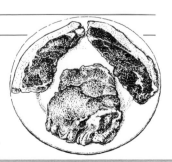

■ COOK'S TIP

Lamb chops are very good cooked on a barbecue, but trim off any excess fat to prevent it dripping on charcoal and flaring.

101 MIXED KEBABS

Preparation time:
10 minutes

Cooking time:
10-15 minutes

Serves 4

Calories:
255 per portion

YOU WILL NEED:
4 rashers rindless, streaky bacon
4 kidneys
1-2 tablespoons oil
1 red pepper, seeded and cut into
*   triangles*
1 green pepper, seeded and cut into
*   triangles*
8 bay leaves
8 cocktail sausages
1 × 227g/8 oz can pineapple slices,
*   drained and cut into chunks*
4 tomatoes, halved
salt and pepper

Cut the bacon rashers in half. Halve the kidneys and snip out the cores. Wrap a piece of bacon round each piece of kidney. Brush four skewers with oil, then thread each one, rotating the ingredients as shown in the photograph. Brush lightly with oil and sprinkle over the salt and pepper.

Cook the kebabs under a hot grill for 10-15 minutes, or until cooked, turning and brushing with extra oil occasionally.

Serve the kebabs hot with boiled potatoes, garnished with chopped parsley, or boiled white rice and a crisp green salad.

102 MEATBALLS AND PEANUT SAUCE

Preparation time:
15 minutes

Cooking time:
8-10 minutes

Serves 4

Calories:
490 per portion

YOU WILL NEED:
450 g/1 lb minced beef
1 onion, grated
salt and pepper
50 g/2 oz fresh white breadcrumbs
1 egg, lightly beaten
1 tablespoon chopped parsley
2 tablespoons plain flour
2 tablespoons oil
1 garlic clove, crushed
2 tablespoons crunchy peanut butter
150 ml/¼ pint natural yogurt
1 teaspoon chilli powder
pinch of cayenne
1 teaspoon chopped parsley, to
*   garnish*

Mix together the meat, onion, seasoning, breadcrumbs, egg and parsley. Form the mixture into 18 small balls the size of marbles and roll in the flour. Combine the oil and the crushed garlic and brush over the meatballs. Thread the meatballs on to oiled skewers and grill for 2-3 minutes, turn the skewers and grill for a further 2-3 minutes.

Melt the peanut butter over a gentle heat, add the remaining ingredients and cook gently until hot, but do not let it boil. Serve the meatballs on a bed of salad. Serve the sauce separately, garnished with parsley.

■ COOK'S TIP

For a change, serve the kebabs with hot lemon and herb bread. Work 2 teaspoons lemon juice and 1 tablespoon chopped parsley into 100 g/4 oz butter. Slice a stick of French bread almost through. Butter both sides of each slice, and press together. Bake in a moderately hot oven for 20 minutes.

■ COOK'S TIP

A food processor 'minces' meat well. Use lean stewing or braising beef and cut into cubes before placing in machine. Try a mixture of beef and pork.

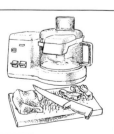

103 SPICY BURGERS

Preparation time:
10 minutes

Cooking time:
4-6 minutes

Serves 4

Calories:
300 per portion

YOU WILL NEED:
450 g/1 lb minced beef, lamb or pork
1 onion, grated
2 garlic cloves, crushed
1 green chilli, seeded and finely chopped (optional)
salt and pepper
oil for frying

Mix together the meat, onion, garlic, the chilli, if using, and seasoning to taste. Shape the mixture into eight burgers. Heat the oil in a frying pan and cook the burgers for 2-3 minutes on either side.

Serve the burgers in baps with lettuce, tomato slices and sweetcorn relish, garnished with tomato wedges, baby gherkins and lettuce. Alternatively, serve with mashed potatoes and Ratatouille (see recipe 115).

104 KEBABS

Preparation time:
15 minutes, plus 2 hours to marinate

Cooking time:
10-12 minutes

Serves 4

Calories:
310 per portion

YOU WILL NEED:
450 g/1 lb boned leg, fillet or shoulder of lamb
2 tablespoons olive oil
juice of 1 lemon
1 teaspoon dried marjoram
salt and pepper
4 button onions
8 cherry tomatoes, or 4 quartered tomatoes
8 button mushrooms
1 green pepper, seeded and cut into squares
8 bay leaves

Cut the lamb into 2.5 cm/1 inch cubes and place in a glass or earthenware dish.

To make the marinade: mix together the oil, lemon juice, marjoram and salt and pepper. Pour the marinade over the lamb, cover and chill for about 2 hours, basting the lamb with the marinade occasionally.

Drain the meat, reserving the marinade. Thread the meat and vegetables on to four oiled skewers alternating the ingredients.

Brush the kebabs with the reserved marinade and grill for about 10-12 minutes. Turn two or three times during cooking and brush with extra marinade if necessary.

Serve the kebabs immediately, accompanied by parslied boiled rice and a crisp mixed salad.

■ COOK'S TIP

For a low-calorie meal use lean minced beef and serve burgers on thick slices of Iceberg or Webb's lettuce. Top with low-calorie salad dressing.

■ COOK'S TIP

These kebabs are excellent cooked on a barbecue. You can use any lean meat or even cubes of firm white fish such as monkfish.

VEGETABLES & SALADS

Vegetables add colour, flavour and texture to the main course of a meal and should be chosen with this in mind to complement the meat or fish dish. Braised or saucy vegetables go well with grills, brightly coloured peppers or tomatoes look attractive with white fish and a crunchy salad adds texture to minced meat dishes.

105 BAKED POTATOES

Preparation time:
15 minutes

Cooking time:
1½ hours

Oven temperature:
200 C, 400 F, gas 6

Serves 4

Calories:
355 per portion

YOU WILL NEED:
4 large baking potatoes
1-2 tablespoons oil
½ teaspoon salt
FOR TOPPING 1
175 g/6 oz cottage cheese
2 tablespoons chopped chives
salt and pepper
FOR TOPPING 2
100 g/4 oz peeled cooked prawns
salt and pepper
50 g/2 oz Cheddar cheese, grated
parsley sprigs, to garnish

Wash the potatoes and prick them with a fork. Brush the oil all over the potatoes and sprinkle a pinch of salt on each. Bake in a moderately hot oven for about 1½ hours or until soft right through to the centre.

Mix the cottage cheese and chives with seasoning to taste. Mix the prawns with seasoning to taste.

When the potatoes are cooked, slit them almost in half and spoon the chosen filling into the cut. Sprinkle the Cheddar over the prawns and heat quickly under the grill. Serve at once.

106 DUCHESSE POTATOES

Preparation time:
15 minutes

Cooking time:
45 minutes

Oven temperature:
200 C, 400 F, gas 6

Serves 4

Calories:
255 per portion

YOU WILL NEED:
675 g/1½ lb potatoes
salt and pepper
50 g/2 oz butter or margarine
1 egg, plus beaten egg to glaze
parsley sprigs, to garnish

Peel and quarter the potatoes. Cook the potatoes in boiling salted water for 20 minutes or until tender. Drain and mash. Beat in the butter or margarine, egg and seasoning. Set aside until cool enough to pipe.

Fit a piping bag with a large star nozzle. Place the potato mixture in the piping bag and pipe rosettes on to a greased baking tray.

Brush the rosettes with the beaten egg and bake in a moderately hot oven for 25 minutes or until golden. Arrange in a warmed serving dish and garnish with parsley sprigs. Serve immediately.

■ MICROWAVE TIP

One to four whole potatoes microwave well. Place them on a double piece of absorbent kitchen paper. Allow about 5, 10, 15 or 20 minutes for 1-4 potatoes.

■ FREEZER TIP

These can be frozen uncooked. Pipe on greaseproof paper. Freeze on the trays until solid, then pack in rigid containers.

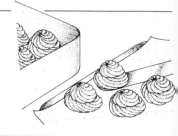

107 FANTAIL POTATOES

Preparation time:
15 minutes, plus 2
hours for soaking

Cooking time:
1 hour

Oven temperature:
190 C, 375 F, gas 5

Serves 4

Calories:
280 per portion

YOU WILL NEED:
4 medium potatoes
2 tablespoons lemon juice
50 g/2 oz butter or margarine
1 onion, finely chopped
1 garlic clove, crushed (optional)
salt and pepper
50 g/2 oz Cheddar cheese, finely
  grated
parsley sprig, to garnish

Peel the potatoes and slice thinly into vertical slices, leaving them attached at the base. Soak the potatoes in a bowl of water with the lemon juice for 2 hours or until the potatoes have fanned out. Drain.

Mix together the melted butter or margarine, the onion, garlic, if using, and seasoning. Place the potatoes in a baking tin, pour over the butter mixture and bake in a moderately hot oven for 50 minutes, basting occasionally. Sprinkle the Cheddar on each potato and bake for a further 10-15 minutes or until the potatoes are crisp and golden. Serve immediately, garnished with a sprig of parsley.

108 LYONNAISE POTATOES

Preparation time:
15 minutes

Cooking time:
25 minutes

Serves 4

Calories:
235 per portion

YOU WILL NEED:
675 g/1½ lb potatoes
salt
50 g/2 oz butter or margarine
2-3 small onions, sliced into rings
chopped parsley, to garnish

Peel and cook the potatoes whole in plenty of boiling salted water for 15 minutes. Drain and cool. Slice the potatoes evenly. Fry the potato slices in the butter or margarine until crisp and golden. When two-thirds cooked, add the onion rings and continue cooking until they are softened.

Garnish with chopped parsley and serve immediately.

■ MICROWAVE TIP

*Microwave these 10-12
minutes on full power.
Cook the butter, onion and
garlic separately 5 minutes,
pour over the potatoes,
sprinkle with cheese. Grill.*

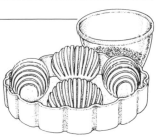

■ MICROWAVE TIP

*Put the raw sliced potatoes
in a serving dish with the
onions. Cover and
microwave on high for
about 30 minutes, stirring
several times.*

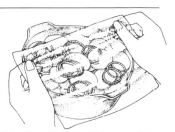

109 BUTTERED CARROTS

Preparation time:
10 minutes

Cooking time:
15-20 minutes

Serves 4

Calories:
150 per portion

YOU WILL NEED:
1 kg/2 lb carrots
salt and pepper
50 g/2 oz butter
chopped parsley, to garnish

Peel the carrots and cut into four lengthways, then cut each quarter into 5 cm/2 inch strips. Bring a saucepan of salted water to the boil and cook the carrots for 10 minutes. Drain well.

Heat the butter gently in a large frying pan. Cook the carrots in the butter for 5 minutes until tender. Season to taste and garnish with chopped parsley.

110 CAULIFLOWER CHEESE

Preparation time:
15 minutes

Cooking time:
40 minutes

Serves 4

Calories:
215 per portion

YOU WILL NEED:
1 medium cauliflower
FOR THE CHEESE SAUCE
25 g/1 oz butter or margarine
25 g/1 oz plain flour
300 ml/½ pint milk
75 g/3 oz Cheddar cheese, grated
¼ teaspoon mustard powder
   (optional)
salt and pepper
¼ teaspoon grated nutmeg, to garnish
   (optional)

Trim the cauliflower, cut a cross in the stem and cook in boiling salted water for about 15 minutes. Drain thoroughly, place on a serving plate and keep hot.

To make the sauce, melt the butter or margarine over a gentle heat, stir in the flour and cook for 2 minutes. Gradually add the milk, stirring all the time. Bring the sauce to the boil, reduce the heat and simmer gently for a few minutes. Remove the saucepan from the heat. Stir the Cheddar into the sauce with the mustard, if using, and seasoning until smooth. Pour the sauce over the cauliflower.

Sprinkle the nutmeg over the top, if liked, and serve immediately.

■ MICROWAVE TIP

Put the prepared carrots and butter in a dish with a sprinkling of water. Cover and microwave on high for about 15 minutes stirring once.

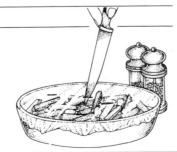

■ MICROWAVE TIP

All sauces cook well in the microwave. Put all the ingredients in a bowl, whisk well and microwave for 8-10 minutes. Whisk thoroughly.

111 LEEKS IN SAUCE

Preparation time:
10 minutes

Cooking time:
20 minutes

Serves 4

Calories:
215 per portion

YOU WILL NEED:
8 medium leeks
salt
FOR THE CHEESE SAUCE
25 g/1 oz butter or margarine
25 g/1 oz plain flour
150 ml/¼ pint milk
75 g/3 oz Cheddar cheese, grated
salt and pepper
pinch of mustard powder

Trim, wash and slice the leeks in half lengthways. Put the leeks in a large saucepan, add a little salt, then pour in enough water to just cover the vegetables. Bring to the boil, then simmer for 10 minutes. Drain the leeks well and reserve 150 ml/¼ pint of the cooking water for the sauce. Place in a serving dish and keep hot.

To make the sauce, melt the butter or margarine over a gentle heat, then stir in the flour and cook for 2 minutes. Gradually add the milk and leek water, stirring the mixture all the time. Bring the sauce to the boil and simmer gently for a few minutes. Remove from the heat, stir in the Cheddar, seasoning and mustard. Mix until smooth and pour the sauce over the leeks. Serve at once.

112 CELERY WITH WALNUTS

Preparation time:
5-10 minutes

Cooking time:
25-30 minutes

Serves 4

Calories:
195 per portion

YOU WILL NEED:
1 large head of celery
1 large onion, chopped
50 g/2 oz butter or margarine
50 g/2 oz walnut halves
300 ml/½ pint chicken stock
few drops of soy sauce

Trim and wash the celery. Cut the sticks in 5 cm/2 inch lengths.

Fry the onion in the butter or margarine in a large pan. Add the celery and walnuts. Cook for a few minutes, then pour in the stock. Simmer uncovered for 25-30 minutes until softened. Season with soy sauce. Serve immediately.

■ COOK'S TIP

Substitute dry white wine for cooking water and use half the quantity of cheese to make a wine sauce. Or use all milk to make a creamy sauce.

■ COOK'S TIP

To keep a head of celery fresh, store it on a cool windowsill with root end in a jug of water.

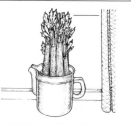

113 BRUSSELS SPROUTS WITH CHESTNUTS

Preparation time:
20 minutes

Cooking time:
20 minutes

Serves 4

Calories:
290 per portion

YOU WILL NEED:
1 kg/2¼ lb Brussels Sprouts
450 g/1 lb chestnuts
50 g/2 oz butter or margarine

Trim the sprouts, removing any damaged outer leaves and cut a cross in the stalks. Slit the chestnut skins, put in cold water in a saucepan and bring to the boil. Boil for 2 minutes, then drain and remove outer and inner skins. (Dried, frozen or canned chestnuts may be used, following the instructions on the packet or can.) Cook the sprouts and chestnuts in boiling salted water for 15 minutes. Drain well.

Heat the butter or margarine in a large frying pan and fry the sprouts and chestnuts together for 5 minutes, tossing well. Serve immediately. This dish is a good accompaniment for Roast Turkey (see recipe 85).

114 COURGETTE FRITTERS

Preparation time:
15 minutes

Cooking time:
5-10 minutes

Serves 4

Calories:
385 per portion

YOU WILL NEED:
450 g/1 lb courgettes
flour to dust
1 × recipe tomato sauce (recipe 161)
chopped parsley, to garnish
FOR THE BATTER
100 g/4 oz plain flour
pinch of salt
1 egg yolk
300 ml/½ pint milk or water (to make a crisper batter)
1 tablespoon oil
oil for deep frying

Trim and slice the courgettes and dust with flour. For the batter sift the flour and salt into a bowl. Make a well in the centre. Add the egg yolk, then gradually beat in the milk and tablespoon oil. Beat until smooth.

Heat the oil for deep frying to 190 C/375 F; test the temperature by dropping a cube of bread into the oil; it should turn golden in 30 seconds. Dip the courgette slices in the batter and drop into the hot oil a few at a time. Fry the fritters for 5 minutes or until golden. Drain on absorbent kitchen paper and keep warm while cooking the remaining courgettes. Serve immediately with tomato sauce and garnish with chopped parsley.

■ MICROWAVE TIP

Brussels sprouts microwave well – prepare and wash them. Cook the wetted sprouts in a roasting bag for about 15 minutes.

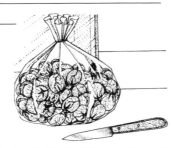

■ COOK'S TIP

To make aubergine fritters, trim and slice two large aubergines. Salt them for 30 minutes, then rinse and dry well. Dust with flour and cook as above.

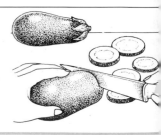

115 RATATOUILLE

Preparation time:
15 minutes

Cooking time:
20-25 minutes

Serves 4

Calories:
235 per portion

YOU WILL NEED:
1 aubergine
salt and pepper
2 meduim onions
2 courgettes
1 red pepper
1 green pepper
675 g/1½ lb tomatoes
4-6 tablespoons oil
2 garlic cloves, crushed
¼ teaspoon dried mixed herbs

Thinly slice the aubergine, place in a colander and sprinkle generously with salt to remove the bitter flavour. Leave to drain while preparing the other vegetables. Thinly slice the onions and courgettes. Core, seed and slice the peppers. Peel, quarter and seed the tomatoes.

Heat the oil in a large saucepan. Cook the onion with the garlic until softened. Rinse and dry the aubergine slices and add to the pan with the remaining vegetables, herbs and seasoning. Bring the mixture to the boil, reduce the heat and simmer gently, covered, for 15-20 minutes. Stir the vegetables from time to time during cooking to ensure that the juices are evenly mixed.

116 CHILLI-STUFFED PEPPERS

Preparation time:
15 minutes

Cooking time:
50 minutes

Oven temperature:
180 C, 350 F, gas 4

Serves 4

Calories:
375 per portion

YOU WILL NEED:
4 green peppers, tops reserved and
  seeded
FOR THE FILLING
1 onion, chopped
1 garlic clove, crushed
350 g/12 oz minced beef
1 tablespoon oil
100 g/4 oz mushrooms, sliced
2 teaspoons chilli powder
1 tablespoon tomato purée
150 ml/¼ pint beef stock
salt and pepper
1 × 425 g/15 oz can kidney beans

Blanch the peppers in boiling salted water for 1-2 minutes and drain. Place in an ovenproof dish.

Fry the onion, garlic and minced beef in the oil until browned. Stir in the mushrooms, chilli powder, tomato purée, stock and seasoning and simmer gently for 10 minutes. Drain the kidney beans and add to the meat.

Fill the peppers with the chilli mixture, cover the dish and bake in a moderate oven for 30 minutes.

■ COOK'S TIP

Ratatouille makes a refreshing starter – cut the vegetables into chunks instead of slices. Cook and cool, then chill and serve with warm French bread.

■ COOK'S TIP

If you find a whole pepper too much for 1 serving, then cut 2 peppers in half lengthways to make boat shapes. Place in a baking dish and pile the filling in.

117 STUFFED MARROW RINGS

Preparation time:
5-10 minutes

Cooking time:
55 minutes

Oven temperature:
190 C, 375 F, gas 5

Serves 4

Calories:
440 per portion

YOU WILL NEED:
1 onion, chopped
1 tablespoon oil
450 g/1 lb minced beef
1 × 400 g/14 oz can chopped
  tomatoes
50 g/2 oz flaked almonds
50 g/2 oz sultanas
1 teaspoon ground cinnamon
1 teaspoon grated nutmeg
salt and pepper
4 × 5 cm/2 inch thick slices marrow,
  peeled
parsley sprig, to garnish

Fry the onion in the oil until softened and transparent. Add the minced beef and cook until browned, stirring briskly. Add the remaining ingredients, except the marrow slices, bring the mixture to the boil and simmer until thickened, about 15 minutes.

Meanwhile, scoop out the seeds from the marrow slices, leaving a hole in the centre of each slice. Arrange the rings in a baking dish.

Pour the meat mixture into the centre of each marrow slice and pile the remainder on top. Cover the dish with foil and bake in a moderately hot oven for 30 minutes or until the marrow is tender.

Transfer to a serving plate, garnish with a sprig of parsley, and serve immediately with baked potatoes.

118 HOT SPRING SALAD

Preparation time:
10 minutes

Cooking time:
15 minutes

Serves 4

Calories:
370 per portion

YOU WILL NEED:
675 g/1½ lb fresh spinach
4 slices bread, crusts removed, cut
  into cubes
50 g/2 oz butter, or 15 g/½ oz butter
  and 2 tablespoons oil
8 rashers rindless streaky bacon, diced
100 g/4 oz button mushrooms, whole
3 tablespoons oil
2 garlic cloves, crushed
1 tablespoon wine vinegar
¼ teaspoon mustard powder
salt and pepper

Wash and shred the spinach. Place in a large salad bowl. Fry the bread cubes in the butter, or butter and oil mixture, until golden. Remove, drain on absorbent kitchen paper, then sprinkle the cubes over the spinach. Fry the bacon in any remaining fat until really crispy. Add the mushrooms and continue cooking for a few minutes.

Mix the remaining ingredients together and pour over the mushrooms and bacon. Bring the mixture quickly to the boil, pour over the spinach and toss gently. Serve at once.

■ COOK'S TIP

Use the meat mixture to stuff courgettes. Cut 4 large courgettes in half lengthways. Scoop out the middle and fill with the mixture. Bake as above.

■ COOK'S TIP

Use flavoured vinegars in salads. Put herb sprigs – tarragon, thyme, basil, rosemary – into white wine vinegar and leave for 1 month before use.

119 CHICKEN AND RICE SALAD

Preparation time:
35 minutes

Cooking time:
25 minutes

Serves 4

Calories:
400 per portion

YOU WILL NEED:
225 g/8 oz long-grain rice
600 ml/1 pint water
salt and pepper
450 g/1 lb cooked chicken
2 tablespoons mayonnaise
150 ml/¼ pint soured cream
1 tablespoon curry powder
1 tablespoon oil
1 tablespoon chutney
coriander leaves, to garnish

Put the rice in a saucepan with the water, and a little salt. Bring to the boil, cover and reduce the heat. Simmer for about 20 minutes or until the rice is cooked and all the water has been absorbed. Fluff up the grains with a fork and leave to cool.

Arrange the rice in the base and to form a border round the rim of a serving dish. Dice the chicken and place in a bowl. Cook the curry powder in the oil for 2-3 minutes, cool and mix with the remaining ingredients, seasoning with salt and pepper to taste. Toss with the chicken and spoon over the rice.

Garnish with fresh coriander leaves just before serving. Accompany with a green salad.

120 CHEESE AND SALAMI SALAD

Preparation time:
15 minutes, plus 30 minutes to chill

Serves 4

Calories:
330 per portion

YOU WILL NEED:
100 g/4 oz Gruyère cheese
100 g/4 oz Edam cheese
100 g/4 oz salami, sliced
6-8 black olives
50 g/2 oz cocktail gherkins
chopped chives, to garnish

Dice the Gruyère and Edam cheeses into 1 cm/½ inch cubes. Cut a slit in each piece of salami from the centre to the edge and roll to form a cone. Arrange the cheeses and salami cones on a serving dish. Halve and stone the black olives and add them to the dish with the cocktail gherkins.

Chill for about 30 minutes. Serve garnished with chopped fresh chives.

■ MICROWAVE TIP

Rice in the microwave: put 225 g/8 oz rice, 600 ml/1 pint water and ½ teaspoon salt in a large bowl. Cook 15 minutes. Stand for 5 minutes.

■ COOK'S TIP

Flavour bottled mayonnaise with tomato purée, Worcestershire sauce, garlic salt and paprika. Thin with cream or yogurt to serve with this salad.

121 CHEESE AND FRUIT SALAD

Preparation time:
15 minutes, plus
time to chill

Serves 4

Calories:
290 per portion

YOU WILL NEED:
small head of Chinese leaves, shredded
1 × 227g/8 oz can pineapple chunks
100 g/4 oz cottage cheese
100 g/4 oz Cheddar cheese, diced
100 g/4 oz cooked ham, diced
salt and pepper
1 avocado
1 tablespoon lemon juice

Arrange the Chinese leaves in the bottom of a serving dish.
Drain the pineapple chunks. Mix with the cottage cheese,
Cheddar and ham. Season well and spoon the mixture on top
of the leaves.

Halve the avocado. Scoop out the stone, then peel and
thinly slice. Sprinkle with lemon juice and arrange the slices
on top of the cheese mixture. Chill before serving.

122 SMOKED MACKEREL AND EGG SALAD

Preparation time:
15 minutes

Serves 4

Calories:
335 per portion

YOU WILL NEED:
1 lettuce, shredded
2 smoked mackerel fillets
4 hard-boiled eggs
4 tomatoes, peeled and quartered
FOR THE DRESSING
1 tablespoon wine vinegar
2 tablespoons oil
1 teaspoon prepared French mustard
salt and pepper
1 tablespoon chopped parsley

Put the lettuce in a serving bowl. Skin and flake the mackerel.
Roughly chop the hard-boiled eggs. Mix together the mackerel, eggs and tomatoes and arrange on top of the lettuce.

Combine the ingredients for the dressing and pour over
the fish. Serve immediately.

■ COOK'S TIP

*If you're counting the
calories, omit the avocado.
Use fruit canned in
unsweetened juice, low-fat
Cheddar and lean ham.*

■ COOK'S TIP

*In Spring thin out young
lettuce plants to use in this
salad. Use horseradish sauce
instead of the mustard to
pep up the salad.*

123 WALDORF SALAD

Preparation time:
10-15 minutes

Serves 4

Calories:
140 per portion

YOU WILL NEED:
1 lettuce
2 red dessert apples
2 tart green dessert apples
4 celery sticks
50 g/2 oz walnut halves
150 ml/¼ pint natural yogurt
½ teaspoon sugar
1 teaspoon prepared mustard
salt and pepper

Shred the lettuce and place in a salad bowl. Halve, core and cut the apples into triangles or cubes, cutting and reserving a few slices for garnish. Chop the celery.

Mix together the apples, celery, walnuts, yogurt, sugar, mustard and seasoning and turn into the salad bowl on top of the lettuce. Top with a walnut and apple slices and serve to accompany cold meats.

124 PEANUT COLESLAW

Preparation time:
15 minutes

Serves 4

Calories:
370 per portion

YOU WILL NEED:
½ small white cabbage
1 onion
4 carrots
2 tart dessert apples
50 g/2 oz salted peanuts
150 ml/¼ pint mayonnaise
1 tablespoon lemon juice
salt and pepper

Core and finely shred the cabbage. Halve and thinly slice the onion. Peel and coarsely grate the carrots. Peel, core and coarsely grate the apples. Place all the ingredients in a mixing bowl and toss well.

Turn the coleslaw into a serving dish and serve to accompany cold meats and flans.

■ COOK'S TIP

Nuts add texture interest as well as flavour to salads. They also provide protein. Try hazelnuts, pecans, brazils, peanuts and almonds in salads.

■ COOK'S TIP

Make a delicious supper with coleslaw and grilled bacon rolls in buttered French bread.

125 GREEN SALAD

Preparation time:
10-15 minutes

Serves 4

Calories:
120 per portion

YOU WILL NEED:
1 lettuce
¼ cucumber
1 green pepper
POSSIBLE ADDITIONS
4 spring onions
bunch of watercress
FOR THE FRENCH DRESSING
1 tablespoon wine vinegar
3 tablespoons olive oil
1 teaspoon mustard powder
½ teaspoon sugar
salt and pepper

Separate the lettuce into leaves and arrange in a large salad bowl. Thinly slice the cucumber. Core, seed and slice the pepper into rings. Chop the spring onions, if using, and remove the stalks from the watercress; separate into small sprigs. Scatter the salad vegetables over the lettuce.

To make the dressing, put all the ingredients in a screw-topped jar, shake well and pour over the salad. Serve immediately.

126 MUSHROOM SALAD

Preparation time:
10 minutes, plus 30 minutes to chill

Serves 4

Calories:
115 per portion

YOU WILL NEED:
450 g/1 lb button mushrooms
FOR THE DRESSING
2 garlic cloves, crushed
3 tablespoons oil
1 tablespoon lemon juice
salt and pepper
2 tablespoons chopped fresh mint

Wipe the mushrooms and place in a serving bowl. Mix the dressing ingredients together well. Pour over and toss the mushrooms in the dressing.

Chill for at least 30 minutes before serving.

■ COOK'S TIP

If the variety of green salad ingredients is limited add lots of coarsely chopped parsley for a fresh taste.

■ COOK'S TIP

Scoop out bread rolls, brush all over with melted butter or margarine and bake until crisp. Serve the salad in the cooled rolls to make a delicious starter.

127 TOMATO AND ONION SALAD

Preparation time:
10 minutes

Serves 4

Calories:
170 per portion

YOU WILL NEED:
8 tomatoes
2 onions
coriander or parsley sprig, to garnish
FOR THE DRESSING
4 tablespoons olive oil
1 tablespoon wine vinegar
pinch of mustard powder
1 teaspoon sugar
1 tablespoon chopped fresh herbs, for example, coriander, parsley, and basil
salt and pepper

Thinly slice the tomatoes and onions, and arrange in a serving dish.

To make the dressing, put all the ingredients in a screw-topped jar and shake well. Pour the dressing over the tomato and onion. Garnish with a sprig of coriander or parsley.

128 POTATO SALAD

Preparation time:
10 minutes

Cooking time:
15 minutes

Serves 4

Calories:
345 per portion

YOU WILL NEED:
675 g/1½ lb potatoes
150 ml/¼ pint mayonnaise
2 tablespoons single cream
2-3 tablespoons chopped chives
salt and pepper

Use small, new potatoes when in season; leave the skins on and scrub clean. If using old potatoes, peel and cut into chunks. Cook in a pan of boiling salted water for 15 minutes, or until tender. Drain and allow to cool.

Mix together the remaining ingredients; pour over the potatoes and mix well. Place the potato salad in a serving bowl and serve with cold meats or a quiche.

■ COOK'S TIP

Alternative idea: add grated orange rind to the dressing and use finely chopped fresh rosemary instead of the basil. Good with grilled lamb or pork sausages.

■ COOK'S TIP

Flavour a simple potato salad with chopped black olives, garlic and marjoram. Dress with olive oil and lemon juice for a Mediterranean flavour.

VEGETARIAN RECIPES

Many people are finding that they feel healthier if they cut down on the amount of meat they eat each week and are looking for alternative forms of protein. The recipes in this chapter are for delicious and nutritious meals and snacks using beans, pulses, nuts and seeds. There is a wide variety of dishes suitable for all occasions.

129 VEGETABLE PANCAKES

Preparation time:
30 minutes

Cooking time:
35-40 minutes

Oven temperature:
220 C, 425 F, gas 7

Serves 4

Calories:
425 per portion

YOU WILL NEED:
100 g/4 oz plain flour
salt and pepper
1 egg
300 ml/½ pint milk
oil for frying
1 onion, chopped
1 green pepper, seeded and diced
4 courgettes, diced
1 × 400 g/14 oz can tomatoes
½ teaspoon oregano
1 × recipe cheese sauce (recipe 110)
chopped parsley, to garnish

Sift the flour and pinch of salt into a bowl. Make a well in the centre, add the egg and gradually beat in the milk to make a smooth batter. Lightly oil a crêpe pan or small frying pan. Place over a moderate heat. Pour in about 2 tablespoons of the batter, tilting the pan to coat the base. Cook until golden, turn and cook the second side. Repeat to make about eight large pancakes.

Cook the onion, and pepper in a little oil until softened. Add the courgettes, tomatoes, oregano and seasoning and simmer for 10-15 minutes. Fill the pancakes, roll up and place in an ovenproof dish. Pour over the cheese sauce and bake in a hot oven for 15 minutes. Garnish with parsley and serve with a green salad.

130 VEGETABLE LASAGNE

Preparation time:
55 minutes

Cooking time:
1 hour

Oven temperature:
200 C, 400 F, gas 6

Serves 4

Calories:
650 per portion

YOU WILL NEED:
1 aubergine
salt and pepper
1 onion, chopped
1 green pepper, seeded and cut into
  rings
2 garlic cloves, crushed
oil for frying
4 courgettes, sliced
100 g/4 oz mushrooms, sliced
1 × 400 g/14 oz can tomatoes
½ teaspoon dried basil
225 g/8 oz no-need-to-cook
  wholewheat lasagne
2 × recipe cheese sauce (recipe 110)

Slice the aubergine, place in a colander, sprinkle generously with salt and leave to drain for 30 minutes. Wash, drain and dry well. Fry the onion, pepper and garlic in oil until softened. Add the aubergine and cook until softened. Stir in the courgettes, mushrooms, tomatoes, basil and seasoning.

Layer the lasagne and vegetable mixture in a greased lasagne dish, ending with pasta on top. Pour the sauce over and bake in a moderately hot oven for 45-50 minutes, or until golden and bubbly.

■ COOK'S TIP

Interleave cooked pancakes with absorbent kitchen paper (separate layers in each piece to give fine sheets) to prevent them sticking when stacked.

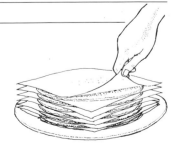

■ COOK'S TIP

To use ordinary dried wholewheat lasagne, cook in plenty of boiling salted water for 15 minutes. Drain, rinse in cold water, then dry on absorbent kitchen paper.

131 SUNFLOWER SEED VEGETABLE BAKE

Preparation time:
20 minutes

Cooking time:
55 minutes

Oven temperature:
200 C, 400 F, gas 6

Serves 4

Calories:
255 per portion

YOU WILL NEED:
450 g/1 lb potatoes, peeled and
    quartered
225 g/8 oz carrots, sliced
salt and pepper
1 onion, chopped
50 g/2 oz sunflower seeds
oil for frying
¼ teaspoon marjoram
2 leeks, sliced into rings
2 garlic cloves, crushed
2 courgettes, sliced
100 g/4 oz mushrooms, sliced
1 tablespoon grated Parmesan cheese
1 tablespoon chopped parsley, to
    garnish

Cook the potatoes and carrots together in boiling salted water. Drain and mash. Fry the onion and sunflower seeds in the oil until the onion is soft. Stir into the potato mixture, add the marjoram and season to taste.

Fry the leeks and garlic in the oil for abut 5 minutes. Season to taste. Add the courgettes and mushrooms and cook for 2-3 minutes.

Put half the leek mixture in an ovenproof dish. Spread half the potato mixture on top. Add the rest of the leek mixture, then top with the remaining potato.

Sprinkle the Parmesan over and bake for 20-25 minutes or until golden. Garnish with parsley.

▉ MICROWAVE TIP

Microwave the potatoes with 2 tablespoons water in a roasting bag 15 minutes. Microwave the remaining vegetables 8-10 minutes. Layer and brown under grill.

132 AUBERGINE AND TOMATO BAKE

Preparation time:
50 minutes

Cooking time:
45 minutes

Oven temperature:
200 C, 400 F, gas 6

Serves 4

Calories:
95 per portion

YOU WILL NEED:
2 aubergines, cubed
salt and pepper
1 onion, chopped
2 garlic cloves, crushed
1-2 tablespoons oil
2 courgettes, diced
1 × 400 g/14 oz can plum tomatoes
1 teaspoon ground cumin
FOR THE TOPPING
50 g/2 oz butter or margarine
100 g/4 oz plain flour
25 g/1 oz unroasted sesame seeds
salt and pepper
knobs of butter

Place the aubergine in a colander, sprinkle with salt and leave to drain for 30 minutes. Rinse, drain and pat dry. Fry the onion and garlic in the oil until soft. Add the aubergine and courgette and fry for a further 5 minutes. Pour in the tomatoes, add the cumin and seasoning and bring to the boil.

Rub the fat into the flour until the mixture resembles fine breadcrumbs. Stir in the sesame seeds and seasoning. Pour the vegetable mixture into an ovenproof dish, spread the crumble mixture on top and dot with the butter. Bake in a moderately hot oven for 30 minutes, or until the top is golden.

▉ COOK'S TIP

Try growing your own garlic – divide a bulb and plant plump individual cloves. Put them in the garden or outside in a pot as they can smell strongly.

133 SAVOURY PUFF

Preparation time:
20 minutes

Cooking time:
45 minutes

Oven temperature:
220 C, 425 F, gas 7
180 C, 350 F, gas 4

Serves 4

Calories:
530 per portion

YOU WILL NEED:
2 small carrots, diced
100 g/4 oz broccoli, separated into
*   florets*
1 small green pepper, seeded and diced
2 leeks, trimmed and sliced into rings
salt and pepper
100 g/4 oz Lancashire cheese, diced
1 teaspoon dill weed
1 × 368 g/13 oz packet frozen puff
*   pastry, defrosted*
beaten egg, to glaze
watercress sprig, to garnish

Cook the prepared vegtables together in boiling salted water for 5 minutes. Drain and plunge into a basin of cold water. Leave for a few minutes in the water, then drain again thoroughly. Mix the vegetables with the cheese, dill weed and seasoning to taste.

Roll out the pastry thinly to make a 30 cm/12 inch square. Place on a greased baking tray. Spoon the filling into the centre of the square. Brush the edges of the pastry with a little water and bring the four corners to the centre, pinching well to seal. Glaze the pastry with beaten egg and garnish with small pastry shapes.

Bake in a hot oven for 15 minutes, then reduce the heat to moderate and cook for a further 30 minutes until golden. Garnish with a sprig of watercress and serve immediately, accompanied with a salad.

134 SPRING ROLLS

Preparation time:
20 minutes

Cooking time:
15-20 minutes

Serves 4

Calories:
280 per portion

YOU WILL NEED:
50 g/2 oz plain flour
salt and pepper
1 egg yolk
150 ml/¼ pint milk
oil for frying, plus extra for deep
*   frying*
1 onion, thinly sliced
1 red pepper, seeded and thinly sliced
100 g/4 oz bean sprouts
½ teaspoon ground ginger
1 tablespoon soy sauce
1-2 egg whites
parsley sprigs, to garnish

Make the pancake batter as instructed in recipe 129, using the egg yolk. Heat a little oil in a small frying pan. Pour in a little batter and tilt the pan so the batter covers the base. Cook until the underside is golden, then turn and lightly brown the second side. Repeat with the remaining batter.

Mix together the vegetables, ginger, soy sauce and seasoning. Place some of this filling in the centre of each pancake. Brush the edges of the pancake with egg white. Roll up, folding in the sides to enclose the filling completely in a neat package. Seal the join with egg white, then brush egg white all over the pancakes.

Heat the oil for deep frying to 190 C/375 F. Fry the rolls for 4-5 minutes or until golden. Drain on absorbent kitchen paper and serve, garnished with parsley and accompanied with tomato sauce (see recipe 161).

■ COOK'S TIP

Look out for ready-rolled puff pastry, sold frozen in thin sheets, and chilled puff pastry. If you prefer to avoid animal fat in your diet, puff pastry made from vegetable *oil is available, and wholemeal puff pastry can also be bought. Any can be used in the above recipe.*

■ FREEZER TIP

Make a large batch of these, fill and brush with egg white. Place on cling film on a baking tray and freeze. Deep fry from frozen as required.

135 LENTIL LOAF

Preparation time:
15 minutes

Cooking time:
1½ hours

Oven temperature:
180 C, 350 F, gas 4

Serves 4

Calories:
390 per portion

YOU WILL NEED:
225 g/8 oz red lentils
600 ml/1 pint boiling water
1 onion, chopped
2 garlic cloves, crushed
1 tablespoon oil
100 g/4 oz fresh brown breadcrumbs
100 g/4 oz Cheddar cheese, grated
1 tablespoon chopped parsley
½ teaspoon dried mixed herbs
1 egg
salt and pepper
halved hazelnuts, to garnish

Line a 1 kg/2 lb loaf tin with greaseproof paper, grease well.

Cook the lentils in the boiling water for about 30 minutes, or until all the water has been absorbed and the lentils are mushy; stir frequently towards the end of the cooking time.

Cook the onion and garlic in the oil until soft. Mix with the lentils and remaining ingredients and season to taste. Pack the lentil mixture into the prepared tin, cover with a sheet of greaseproof paper and bake in a moderate oven for 1 hour. Serve garnished with hazelnuts.

136 VEGETARIAN BURGERS

Preparation time:
15 minutes

Cooking time:
15-20 minutes

Serves 4

Calories:
330 per portion

YOU WILL NEED:
1 onion, grated
675 g/1½ lb white cabbage, grated
225 g/8 oz carrots, grated
100 g/4 oz hazelnuts, coarsely
 chopped
100 g/4 oz fresh brown breadcrumbs
1 large egg
3 tablespoons soy sauce
1 teaspoon marjoram
salt and pepper
25 g/1 oz plain flour
oil for deep frying
parsley sprig, to garnish

Mix together all the ingredients, except the flour, and beat well. Shape the mixture into eight cakes and coat each in the flour.

Heat the oil for deep frying to 190 C/375 F (until a cube of bread turns golden in 30 seconds). Cook the burgers a few at a time for 5-7 minutes, or until golden, and drain on absorbent kitchen paper. Keep hot while cooking the remaining burgers. Garnish with a sprig of parsley and serve hot with Leeks in Sauce (see recipe 111).

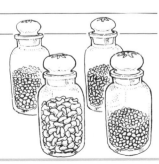

▆ COOK'S TIP

Instead of lentils, try chick peas, haricot beans or butter beans.

▆ FREEZER TIP

These burgers freeze well. Make a large batch, shape and open freeze on cling film until firm. Pack in bags and label. Cook from frozen.

137 POTATO CAKES

Preparation time:
20 minutes, plus 30
minutes to chill

Cooking time:
10-15 minutes

Serves 4

Calories:
400 per portion

YOU WILL NEED:
675 g/1½ lb potatoes, cooked
knob of butter or margarine
1 tablespoon milk
salt and pepper
1 onion, grated
50 g/2 oz Cheddar cheese, grated
2 tablespoons chopped parsley
1 teaspoon mustard powder
flour to coat
1 egg, lightly beaten
100 g/4 oz fresh wholemeal
breadcrumbs
oil for frying
parsley sprig, to garnish

Mash the potatoes with the butter or margarine, milk and sea-soning until smooth. Allow to cool. Mix in the onion, Ched-dar, parsley and mustard. Divide the mixture into eight por-tions, shape into cakes and coat in flour. Dip the cakes in the beaten egg and coat in the breadcrumbs, pressing them on well. Refrigerate for about 30 minutes.

Shallow fry the cakes in oil, a few at a time, for about 2-3 minutes on each side. Drain on absorbent kitchen paper and keep hot while cooking the remaining cakes. Garnish with parsley and serve immediately with a crisp green salad.

138 BAKED STUFFED COURGETTES

Preparation time:
20 minutes

Cooking time:
20 minutes

Oven temperature:
200 C, 400 F, gas 6

Serves 4

Calories:
250 per portion

YOU WILL NEED:
4 large courgettes
1 onion, finely chopped
1 tablespoon oil
50 g/2 oz Lancashire cheese, grated
25 g/1 oz butter
25 g/1 oz plain flour
300 ml/½ pint milk
salt and pepper
2 teaspoons sesame seeds
watercress sprigs, to garnish

Cut the courgettes in half lengthways, scoop out the middle and chop finely.

Cook the onion in the oil until soft. Mix with the chopped courgette and cheese. Melt the butter in a saucepan, stir in the flour and cook for 2 minutes. Gradually add the milk, stirring continuously. Add the courgette and cheese mixture, season to taste with salt and pepper. Spoon the fill-ing into the courgette shells and place in an ovenproof dish.

Sprinkle over the sesame seeds and bake in a moderately hot oven for about 20 minutes. Serve hot, garnished with sprigs of watercress.

■ COOK'S TIP

For a quick alternative substitute instant mashed potato. Add 2 tablespoons grated Parmesan cheese for a good cheesy flavour.

■ COOK'S TIP

For a main dish, cook swedes and carrots together, drain and mash. Pipe between the courgettes, top with grated cheese and bake as above.

139 STUFFED CABBAGE LEAVES

Preparation time:	**YOU WILL NEED:**
20 minutes	*12 large cabbage leaves*
	1 onion, grated
Cooking time:	*2 carrots, grated*
50 minutes	*100 g/4 oz brown rice, cooked*
Oven temperature:	*100 g/4 oz salted peanuts, chopped*
190 C, 375 F, gas 5	*1 egg*
	2 tablespoons soy sauce
Serves 4	*salt and pepper*
Calories:	*150 ml/¼ pint vegetable stock*
340 per portion	*1 × recipe tomato sauce (recipe 161)*

Cut away the stem from each cabbage leaf and blanch the leaves in boiling water. Drain thoroughly and leave to cool.

Mix together the onion, carrot, rice, peanuts, egg, soy sauce and seasoning. Divide the mixture between the cabbage leaves and roll up each leaf, folding in the sides, to enclose the filling in a neat package. Place the stuffed cabbage leaves in an ovenproof dish and pour over the vegetable stock.

Cover and bake in a moderately hot oven for abut 45 minutes. Carefully drain off the stock and serve immediately, accompanied with tomato sauce.

140 VEGETABLE TERRINE

Preparation time:	**YOU WILL NEED:**
25 minutes, plus 2	*75 g/3 oz margarine*
hours to chill	*75 g/3 oz plain flour*
	600 ml/1 pint milk
Cooking time:	*2 eggs, lightly beaten*
1½ hours	*salt and pepper*
Oven temperature:	*225 g/8 oz carrots, chopped*
160 C, 325 F, gas 3	*1 onion, chopped*
	1 tablespoon oil
Serves 4	*300 g/11 oz Cheddar cheese, grated*
Calories:	*bunch of watercress, trimmed*
740 per portion	*¼ cauliflower, lightly cooked*
	225 g/8 oz peas, cooked
	watercress sprigs, to garnish

Line a 1 kg/2 lb loaf tin with greased greaseproof paper.

Melt the margarine, stir in the flour. Add the milk and bring to the boil, stirring. Cool slightly, then beat in the eggs. Season and cool.

Cook the carrots and onion in the oil for 5 minutes. Blend in a liquidizer with a quarter of the sauce, pour into the tin.

Repeat with 225 g/8 oz of the Cheddar, watercress and another quarter of the sauce. Blend the cauliflower with the remaining Cheddar and a third quarter of the sauce. Finally blend the peas and remaining sauce in a liquidizer. Pour into the tin.

Cover the tin with foil and stand in a roasting tin half-full of hot water. Cook in a moderate oven for 1½ hours. Leave to cool. Refrigerate for 1-2 hours before turning out to serve. Garnish as shown.

■ MICROWAVE TIP

Microwave cabbage leaves in a roasting bag with 2 tablespoons water 5 minutes. Microwave assembled dish, covered, on full power 15-20 minutes.

■ MICROWAVE TIP

Layer in a loaf dish (not tin). Cover, microwave on full power for 20 minutes turning occasionally.

141 HUMMOUS

Preparation time:
10 minutes

Serves 4

Calories:
340 per portion

YOU WILL NEED:
1 × 439 g/15½ oz can chick peas,
    drained
1-2 garlic cloves, crushed
grated rind and juice of 1 lemon
2 tablespoons tahini
2 tablespoons mayonnaise
salt and pepper
FOR THE CRUDITES
1 green pepper, seeded and thinly
    sliced
1 red pepper, seeded and thinly sliced
2 carrots, thinly sliced lengthways
2 celery sticks, thinly sliced
chunks of nutty brown bread, to serve

Blend the chick peas, garlic, lemon rind and juice in a liquidizer or food processor until as smooth as possible. Add the
tahini and mayonnaise, 1 tablespoon at a time, blending between each addition. Season well with salt and pepper, pour
the hummus into a small bowl and place on a large serving
plate.

Prepare the vegetables as instructed and arrange with the
bread around the hummus.

142 FRUIT AND VEGETABLE KEBABS

Preparation time:
10 minutes

Cooking time:
10 minutes

Serves 4

Calories:
110 per portion

YOU WILL NEED:
1 courgette, sliced
8 canned pineapple chunks
1 small green pepper, seeded and cut
    into squares
8 canned apricot halves
8 button mushrooms
1 small onion, quartered
4 cherry tomatoes
1 tablespoon oil
salt and pepper

Divide the prepared kebab ingredients equally between four
long skewers and thread on. Mix a little juice from the canned
pineapple with the oil and seasoning, and brush over the
kebabs.

Cook under a hot grill for about 10 minutes, turning and
basting occasionally. Serve hot on a bed of rice and accompany with a green salad.

COOK'S TIP

For a simple starter serve
hummus in scooped out
tomatoes, top each with a
black olive. Serve with hot
pitta bread.

COOK'S TIP

Marinate ingredients in 2
tablespoons chopped herbs,
4 tablespoons oil, garlic salt
and 4 tablespoons orange
juice 2-3 hours. Baste with
marinade during cooking.

143 MIXED BEAN CURRY

Preparation time:
20 minutes, plus
overnight soaking

Cooking time:
1 hour 20 minutes

Serves 4

Calories:
235 per portion

YOU WILL NEED:
100 g/4 oz dried red kidney beans
100 g/4 oz dried black-eye beans
1 onion, chopped
1-2 garlic cloves, crushed
1-2 tablespoons oil
½ teaspoon chilli powder
½ teaspoon ground ginger
1 tablespoon ground cumin
1 tablespoon ground coriander
½ teaspoon turmeric
juice of 1 lemon
1 × 100 g/14 oz can tomatoes
150 ml/¼ pint vegetable stock
salt and pepper
chopped parsley, to garnish

Soak the beans in cold water overnight. Drain and put in a large saucepan. Cover with fresh water and bring to the boil. *Boil rapidly for 10 minutes*, then reduce the heat and simmer for 30 minutes. Drain.

Cook the onion and garlic in the oil until soft. Add the spices and cook over a gentle heat for 2-3 minutes. Add the lemon juice, tomatoes and stock and bring to the boil. Reduce the heat, add the beans and cover the pan. Simmer gently for 30-40 minutes, or until the beans are tender and the excess liquid has been absorbed.

Season to taste, garnish with chopped parsley and serve with brown rice, poppadums and a suitable relish or chutney.

144 VEGETABLE CURRY

Preparation time:
45 minutes

Cooking time:
40 minutes

Serves 4

Calories:
155 per portion

YOU WILL NEED:
1 kg/2 lb mixture of following
vegetables: aubergines, potatoes,
carrots and cauliflower
1 onion, chopped
1-2 garlic cloves, crushed
1-2 tablespoons oil
1 teaspoon ground ginger
1 teaspoon mustard powder
1 teaspoon ground cumin
1 teaspoon ground coriander
2 teaspoons turmeric
300 ml/½ pint vegetable stock
salt and pepper
1 tablespoon coriander leaves

Prepare the vegetables according to type. Cut the aubergine into chunks and put in a colander. Sprinkle with salt and leave for 30 minutes. Drain, rinse and pat dry. Break the cauliflower into florets, roughly chop the carrots and potatoes.

Cook the onion and garlic in the oil until soft. Stir in the spices and cook over a gentle heat for 2 minutes. Add the vegetables and stir well to mix with the fried spices. Stir in the vegetable stock and season with plenty of salt and pepper. Bring to the boil, cover and simmer gently for about 30 minutes. Pour into a warmed serving dish and garnish with chopped coriander. Serve the curry with poppadums and rice.

COOK'S TIP

A spicy egg side dish tastes good with this curry. Roughly chop 4 hard-boiled eggs, sprinkle with chopped onion, chopped fresh coriander and chilli powder.

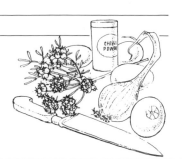

MICROWAVE TIP

Microwave onion, garlic, oil and spices on full power for 5 minutes. Add all ingredients, using hot stock, cover and microwave for 15-20 minutes.

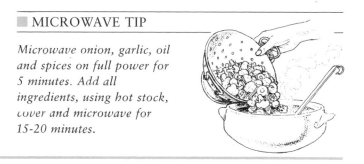

RICE & PASTA

Many of the recipes in this chapter have an international flavour. The imaginative use of flavourings and relatively small quantities of meat or fish has made the rice dishes of the Far East famous throughout the world. Italy is renowned for its delicious pasta dishes, based on many different types of readily available pasta.

145 CHICKEN LIVER RISOTTO

Preparation time:
15 minutes

Cooking time:
30 minutes

Serves 4

Calories:
390 per portion

YOU WILL NEED:
1 onion, chopped
1 red pepper, seeded and chopped
1 green pepper, seeded and chopped
2 carrots, chopped
2 tablespoons oil
225 g/8 oz chicken livers, diced
225 g/8 oz long-grain rice
600 ml/1 pint chicken stock
salt and pepper
chopped watercress, to garnish

In a large frying pan, fry the onions, pepper and carrot in the oil for 5 minutes until soft. Add the chicken livers and cook for a few minutes until browned. Add the rice, stock and seasoning. Bring to the boil and simmer gently for 15-20 minutes, stirring occasionally until cooked.

Serve immediately, garnished with chopped watercress.

146 PAELLA

Preparation time:
15 minutes

Cooking time:
30 minutes

Serves 4

Calories:
650 per portion

YOU WILL NEED:
1 onion, chopped
2 garlic cloves, crushed
1 red pepper, seeded and chopped
3 tablespoons oil
225 g/8 oz long-grain rice
pinch of turmeric
600 ml/1 pint chicken stock
salt and pepper
225 g/8 oz cooked chicken, cut into
*   thick strips*
100 g/4 oz ham, diced
2 chorizo sausages, thickly sliced
100 g/4 oz frozen peas
2 tomatoes, peeled and quartered
100 g/4 oz peeled cooked prawns
1 tablespoon chopped parsley, to
*   garnish*

In a large frying pan, fry the onion, garlic and pepper in the oil for a few minutes until soft.

Add the rice and stir until it is lightly fried and the grains are transparent. Stir in the turmeric, stock and seasoning and simmer, covered, for 15 minutes. Add all the remaining ingredients and cook, covered, for a further 5-10 minutes until almost all the liquid has been absorbed. The paella should be moist.

Sprinkle with the chopped parsley and serve immediately.

■ COOK'S TIP

This is an ideal way of using up cooked chicken or turkey. Add the chopped meat to the risotto when rice is partially cooked.

■ COOK'S TIP

For a delicious and more exotic paella add some firm white fish such as monk fish, haddock or turbot, mussels and squid with the chicken.

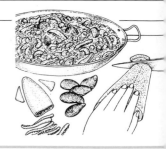

147 BASIC RICE

Preparation time:

Serves 2

Calories:
180 per portion of white, brown, or Basmati rice

YOU WILL NEED:
FOR WHITE RICE
100 g/4 oz long-grain rice
300 ml/½ pint water
salt
FOR BROWN RICE
100 g/4 oz long-grain rice
350 ml/12 fl oz water
salt
FOR BASMATI RICE
100 g/4 oz Basmati rice
scant 300 ml/½ pint water
salt

The method is the same for white and brown rice. Easy-cook varieties do not need washing, but other types of rice should be placed in a sieve and thoroughly rinsed. Put the rice in a saucepan and pour in the water. add a little salt, then bring to the boil. Reduce the heat so that the liquid barely simmers. Give a light stir to make sure the grains are not stuck together and cover the pan.

Simmer very gently, allowing about 15-20 minutes for white rice and about 30-40 minutes for brown rice. At the end of cooking all the liquid should have been absorbed. Fork up the grains and serve.

Basmati rice has a unique and delicate flavour. The grains are quite fragile and starchy. To wash the rice, put it in a basin and pour in cold water to cover. Gently swirl the water with your fingertips, then drain it off. Repeat once or twice until the water runs clear. Cook as white and brown rice, allowing about 25 minutes cooking time.

◼ COOK'S TIP

To keep rice hot for up to 30 minutes, place in a metal colander over an open pan of simmering water. Cover with a tea towel and lid.

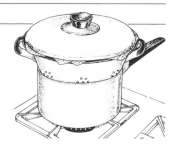

148 PILAU RICE

Preparation time:
10 minutes

Cooking time:
25-30 minutes

Serves 4

Calories:
390 per portion

YOU WILL NEED:
225 g/8 oz Basmati rice
1 onion, choppd
50 g/2 oz butter or margarine
3 cloves
1 × 5 cm/2 on piece cinnamon stick
1 bay leaf
50 g/2 oz flaked almonds
25 g/1 oz raisins
600 ml/1 pint water
salt and pepper

Wash and drain the Basmati rice and set aside. Cook the onion in the butter or margarine in a saucepan until soft. Add the remaining ingredients and bring to the boil. Reduce the heat, cover the pan tightly and simmer gently for 20-25 minutes, or until all the water has been absorbed. Fluff up the rice with a fork and serve immediately.

This is the traditional accompaniment to curry and chicken dishes.

◼ COOK'S TIP

Add a little chopped cooked meat, chicken or fish to the pilau for a light lunch or supper dish.

149 SAFFRON RICE

Preparation time:
5 minutes

Cooking time:
15-20 minutes

Serves 4

Calories:
200 per portion

YOU WILL NEED:
¼ teaspoon saffron strands
600 ml/1 pint water
225 g/8 oz long-grain rice
salt

Put the saffron strands in a pestle and pound them with a mortar until reduced almost to a powder. Stir in a little of the measured water to dissolve the saffron.

Put the rice in a saucepan. (Remember to wash Basmati rice fist, see recipe 147.) Pour in the saffron liquid, rinse the pestle with a little of the measured water to obtain all the colour and flavour. Pour in the rest of the water. Add a pinch of salt and bring to the boil. Reduce the heat, cover and simmer for 15-25 minutes or until all the water has been absorbed. Fluff up the grains with a fork and serve.

150 SAVOURY RICE

Preparation time:
10-15 minutes

Cooking time:
20-25 minutes

Serves 4

Calories:
390 per portion

YOU WILL NEED:
225 g/8 oz long-grain white rice
¼ teaspoon turmeric
600 ml/1 pint water
salt and pepper
1 onion, chopped
1 red pepper, seeded and chopped
1 green pepper, seeded and chopped
100 g/4 oz button mushrooms
1 tablespoon oil
2 peperoni sausages, sliced (optional)
2 tomatoes, peeled and quartered
6 black olives, stoned

Put the rice and turmeric in a saucepan and pour in the water. Add a little salt, then bring to the boil. Reduce the heat so that the liquid barely simmers. Give the rice a light stir to make sure the grains are not stuck together and cover the pan tightly.

Simmer very gently, allowing about 15-20 minutes. At the end of cooking all the liquid should have been absorbed.

Fry the onion, pepper and mushrooms in the oil for 5 minutes until soft. Mix all the ingredients together.

Arrnge the rice attractively on a serving dish and serve hot as an accompaniment, or with a salad as a meal in itself.

■ COOK'S TIP

Add a cinnamon stick or cloves to the water or add chopped fresh herbs such as thyme, dill or parsley to the cooked rice.

■ COOK'S TIP

The vegetables in this recipe can be varied according to what is available. Aubergines, sweetcorn kernels, peas and courgettes are good choices.

151 BROWN RICE RING MOULD

Preparation time:
5-10 minutes, plus
1½ hours to chill

Cooking time:
45 minutes

Serves 4

Calories:
400 per portion

YOU WILL NEED:
225 g/8 oz long grain brown rice
350 ml/12 fl oz water
salt
100 g/4 oz walnut halves, roughly
   chopped
1 × 325 g/12 oz can sweetcorn,
   drained
1 green pepper, seeded and diced
¼ teaspoon paprika
pinch of salt
watercress sprigs, to garnish

Grease a 1.2 litre/2 pint ring mould with oil.

Put the rice in a saucepan and pour in the water. Add a little salt, then bring to the boil. Reduce the heat so that the liquid barely simmers. Give the rice a light stir to make sure the grains are not stuck together and cover the pan tightly.

Simmer very gently for 30-40 minutes. At the end of cooking all the liquid should have been absorbed. Mix all the ingredients together and pack the mixture into the ring mould.

Leave the rice to cool and chill thoroughly. Turn out and serve as an accompaniment to a salad.

152 TOMATO RICE MOULD

Preparation time:
10 minutes

Cooking time:
15-20 minutes

Serves 4

Calories:
295 per portion

YOU WILL NEED:
2 × 400 g/14 oz cans plum tomatoes
2 onions, chopped
1 garlic clove, crushed
1 teaspoon dried or 2 teaspoons
   chopped fresh basil
salt and pepper
225 g/8 oz long-grain white rice
450 ml/¾ pint water
50 g/2 oz Parmesan cheese, grated
watercress sprigs, to garnish

Grease a 1.2 litre/2 pint ring mould with oil.

For the tomato sauce, blend the tomatoes, onion, garlic, basil and seasoning in a liquidizer until smooth. Cook the rice in the tomato sauce and water for 15-20 minutes or until the liquid has evaporated, stirring occasionally. Stir in the Parmesan cheese.

Press the rice into the mould and leave for 5 minutes. Turn out the rice, and serve with a salad or with grilled meat.

■ COOK'S TIP

For a more colourful dish, add peas or diced, peeled and seeded tomatoes to the rice.

■ COOK'S TIP

For a buffet party dish fill centre of rice ring with lightly cooked cauliflower florets tossed in French dressing.

153 RICE CAKES

Preparation time:
10-15 minutes

Cooking time:
25 minutes

Makes 8 cakes

Calories:
370 per portion

YOU WILL NEED:
225 g/8 oz long-grain rice
300 ml/½ pint water
salt and pepper
350 g/12 oz smoked haddock, cod or coley
3 tablespoons oil
1 onion, chopped
grated rind and juice of 1 lemon
2 tablespoons tomato ketchup
2 tablespoons chopped parsley
1 egg

Put the rice in a saucepan and pour in the water. Add a little salt, then bring to the boil. Reduce the heat so that the liquid barely simmers. Give the rice a light stir to make sure the grains are not stuck together and cvoer the pan tightly.

Simmer very gently, allowing about 15-20 minutes for white rice and about 30-40 minutes for brown rice. At the end of cooking all the liquid should have been absorbed.

Place the fish in a frying pan, cover with water and poach for 10 minutes or until the fish is cooked. Skin the fish and remove any bones, then flake the fish.

Heat 1 tablespoon of the oil and cook the onion for a few minutes, then add the rice, fish and remaining ingredients. Mash together well, remove from the heat and form the mixture into cakes. Fry the cakes in the remaining oil until brown, and serve immediately.

154 KEDGEREE

Preparation time:
10 minutes

Cooking time:
30 minutes

Serves 4

Calories:
430 per portion

YOU WILL NEED:
1 onion, chopped
2 tablespoons oil or 25 g/1 oz butter
175 g/6 oz long-grain rice
¼ teaspoon turmeric
450 ml/¾ pint water
225 g/8 oz smoked haddock
50 g/2 oz raisins
50 g/2 oz salted peanuts
3 hard-boiled eggs, roughly chopped
1 tablespoon lemon juice
salt and pepper
1 tablespoon chopped parsley

Cook the onion in the oil or butter until soft but not browned. Add the rice and turmeric, cook for a minute, then pour in the water. Bring to the boil, reduce the heat and cover the pan. Simmer for 15 minutes until the water is absorbed.

Meanwhile, put the smoked haddock in a pan, cover with water and bring to the boil. Reduce the heat and simmer for minutes, or until the fish flakes easily with the point of a knife. Drain and coarsely flake the fish, discarding the skin and any bones.

Add the fish, raisins, peanuts, eggs, lemon juice, seasoning and parsley to the rice. Fork together gently.

Serve the kedgeree immediately.

■ COOK'S TIP

For a quick supper substitute canned pilchards or tuna fish for the smoked fish.

■ COOK'S TIP

For a more spicy kedgeree omit raisins and peanuts and add ¼ teaspoon freshly grated nutmeg.

155 CHICKEN PILAFF WITH APRICOTS

Preparation time:
10 minutes

Cooking time:
20 minutes

Serves 4

Calories:
555 per portion

YOU WILL NEED:
1 onion, chopped
25 g/1 oz butter or margarine
225 g/8 oz long-grain rice
1 kg/2 lb cooked chicken, cut into
 chunks
225 g/8 oz dried apricots, cut in half
600 ml/1 pint chicken stock
¼ teaspoon mixed spice
salt and pepper
natural yogurt, to serve

In a large saucepan cook the onion in the butter or margarine for a few minutes until soft and transparent. Add the rice and stir well until evenly coated in the fat. Add the remaining ingredients, bring the mixture to the boil and simmer gently for 15 minutes or until all the liquid has evaporated.

Serve hot with natural yogurt.

156 RICE BAKE

Preparation time:
25 minutes

Cooking time:
45 minutes

Oven temperature:
200 C, 400 F, gas 6

Serves 4

Calories:
700 per portion

YOU WILL NEED:
100 g/4 oz long-grain rice
300 ml/½ pint water
salt and pepper
225 g/8 oz cooked ham, diced
4 hard-boiled eggs, chopped
225 g/8 oz Cheddar cheese, diced
bunch of parsley, chopped
FOR THE WHITE SAUCE
50 g/2 oz butter or margarine
50 g/2 oz plain flour
600 ml/1 pint milk
salt and pepper

Cook the rice as instructed in recipe 147.

Mix together the ham, eggs, Cheddar, parsley and seasoning, reserving a little parsley to garnish. For the white sauce, melt the butter or margarine over a low heat. Add the flour, cook for 2 minutes, stirring constantly, then gradually add the milk and stir until the sauce boils and thickens. Reduce the heat and simmer gently for 2 minutes. Add the seasoning.

Pour some of the sauce into a baking dish, followed by a layer of ham mixture, then a layer of rice. Continue layering in this fashion until all the ingredients are used up. Finish with a layer of sauce.

Bake in a moderately hot oven for 30 minutes until golden. Garnish with the reserved parsley, and serve hot with a green salad.

■ MICROWAVE TIP

Pilaff reheats particularly well in a microwave. Cover with microwave cling film and heat on full power for 4-5 minutes.

■ FREEZER TIP

Left-over rice freezes well. Pack in a polythene bag and seal. Defrost in a microwave or empty into a pan of boiling water and bring back to the boil.

157 MACARONI CHEESE

Preparation time:	YOU WILL NEED:
15 minutes	225 g/8 oz macaroni
	pinch of salt
Cooking time:	FOR THE CHEESE SAUCE
15-20 minutes	50 g/2 oz butter or margarine
	40 g/1½ oz plain flour
Serves 4	600 ml/1 pint milk
	salt and pepper
Calories:	175 g/6 oz Cheddar cheese, grated
615 per portion	

Put the macaroni into a large saucepan of salted boiling water and simmer gently for 10-15 minutes, until just tender. Drain and set aside.

Melt the butter or margarine in a saucepan over a low heat, then add the flour. Cook for 2 minutes, stirring. Gradually add the milk, and bring the sauce to the boil, stirring constantly. Simmer gently for 2-3 minutes. Remove from the heat, and season well with salt and pepper.

Add the cooked macaroni and 150 g/5 oz of the Cheddar to the sauce and combine well. Pour the mixture into a 1.2 litre/2 pint serving dish and sprinkle the remaining cheese over the top. Brown under a hot grill and serve immediately.

158 LASAGNE VERDI

Preparation time:	YOU WILL NEED:
25 minutes	1 onion, chopped
	2 garlic cloves, crushed
Cooking time:	1 tablespoon oil
1 hour	450 g/1 lb minced beef
Oven temperature:	100 g/4 oz mushrooms, wiped and
200 C, 400 F, gas 6	sliced
	3 tablespoons tomato purée
Serves 4	150 ml/¼ pint beef stock
	¼ teaspoon dried basil
Calories:	¼ teaspoon dried oregano
900 per portion	salt and pepper
	2 × recipe cheese sauce (recipe 110),
	using 75 g/3 oz Cheddar and 75 g/3
	oz mozzarella cheese
	225 g/8 oz no-need-to-cook green
	lasagne

Fry the onions and garlic in the oil for 5 minutes until soft. Add the minced beef and cook for 5 minutes or until browned. Add the mushrooms, tomato purée, stock, basil, oregano, salt and pepper. Bring to the boil, reduce the heat and simmer gently for 20 minutes, stirring occasionally.

Spread a layer of the meat mixture over the bottom of a baking dish, followed by a layer of lasagne. Continue in this fashion until the meat mixture and the lasagne have been used up. Top with the cheese sauce.

Bake in a moderately hot oven for 30 minutes or until golden. Serve hot with garlic bread and a green salad.

■ FREEZER TIP

Grate small left-over pieces of hard cheese and keep in a polythene bag in the freezer to use in cooking.

■ FREEZER TIP

To freeze lasagne, assemble dish but freeze before baking. Cook from frozen for 50-60 minutes until hot and golden.

159 STUFFED CANNELLONI

Preparation time: 15-20 minutes	YOU WILL NEED: 8 cannelloni tubes
	salt and pepper
Cooking time: 1 hour	2 onions, chopped
	2 garlic cloves, crushed
Oven temperature: 180 C, 350 F, gas 4	2 green peppers, seeded and chopped
	1 tablespoon oil
Serves 4	1 × 400 g/14 oz can chopped tomatoes
Calories: 750 per portion	225 g/8 oz corned beef
	½ teaspoon dried or 1 tablespoon chopped fresh basil
	2 × recipe cheese sauce (recipe 110)
	25 g/1 oz Parmesan cheese, grated

Cook the cannelloni in a saucepan of boiling salted water for 10 minutes until just tender. Drain and set aside.

For the filling, fry the onion, garlic and peppers in the oil for 5 minutes until soft. Add the tomatoes and simmer gently for 15 minutes until thickened. Cut the corned beef into small cubes and add to the sauce. Add the seasoning and basil and simmer for a further 5 minutes. Allow the meat mixture to cool slightly. Fill the cannelloni tubes with the meat mixture, then arrange the filled cannelloni in a greased ovenproof dish.

Pour the sauce over the cannelloni, sprinkle over the Parmesan and bake uncovered in a moderate oven for 30 minutes or until the top is crisp and golden.

160 SPAGHETTI BOLOGNESE

Preparation time: 15 minutes	YOU WILL NEED: 1 onion, chopped
	1 garlic clove, crushed
Cooking time: 40-50 minutes	1 tablespoon oil
	450 g/1 lb minced beef
Serves 4	100 g/4 oz mushrooms, sliced
Calories: 525 per portion	1 × 400 g/14 oz can chopped tomatoes
	300 ml/½ pint beef stock
	¼ teaspoon dried or ½ teaspoon finely chopped fresh basil
	salt and pepper
	225 g/8 oz spaghetti
	grated Parmesan cheese, to serve

Fry the onion and garlic in the oil for 5 minutes until soft. Add the mince and continue cooking for 5 minutes or until the meat is browned. Add the mushrooms, tomatoes, stock, basil, salt and pepper to the mince. Bring the mixture to the boil, reduce the heat and simmer gently for 30 minutes or until reduced, stirring occasionally.

Meanwhile, cook the spaghetti in a saucepan of boiling salted water for 10-12 minutes until just tender. Drain and pile the spaghetti into a large serving dish. Pour the Bolognese sauce on top, sprinkle with the Parmesan and serve immediately with a green salad.

■ COOK'S TIP

To fill cannelloni tubes easily, put meat mixture into a piping bag, fitted with a 1-cm/½-in plain nozzle and pipe mixture into cannelloni.

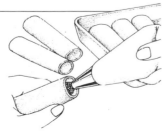

■ FREEZER TIP

Bolognese sauce freezes well. It is worth making double or treble the quantity and storing in two or three portions in the freezer.

161 SPAGHETTI WITH TOMATO SAUCE

Preparation time:	YOU WILL NEED:
5 minutes	1 onion, finely chopped
	2 garlic cloves, crushed
Cooking time:	1 tablespoon oil
25 minutes	1 × 400 g/14 oz can chopped
	tomatoes
Serves 4	½ teaspoon dried or 1 teaspoon
	chopped fresh basil
Calories:	salt and pepper
480 per portion	450 g/1 lb spaghetti

Fry the onion and garlic in the oil for 5 minutes until soft. Add the tomatoes, basil, salt and pepper. Bring to the boil, reduce the heat and simmer gently for 15 minutes or until thickened.

While the sauce is simmering, cook the spaghetti in a large pan of boiling salted water for 10-12 minutes until just tender. Drain, place in a serving bowl and keep hot.

Blend the sauce in a liquidizer. Reheat in a saucepan for a few minutes, pour over the spaghetti and serve immediately.

162 SPAGHETTI WITH WATERCRESS AND WALNUT SAUCE

Preparation time:	YOU WILL NEED:
10 minutes	450 g/1 lb wholewheat spaghetti
	salt and pepper
Cooking time:	1 onion, chopped
15 minutes	1-2 garlic cloves, crushed
	1 tablespoon oil
Serves 4	50 g/2 oz mushrooms, sliced
	50 g/2 oz chopped walnuts
Calories:	bunch of watercress, chopped
615 per portion	300 ml/½ pint soured cream

Cook the spaghetti in a large pan of boiling salted water for 10-12 minutes until just tender.

Meanwhile, make the sauce. Cook the onion and garlic in the oil until transparent. Add the mushrooms and walnuts and cook for a further few minutes. Remove the pan from the heat, stir in the watercress, soured cream and seasoning. Reheat very gently – do not allow the sauce to boil or the cream will curdle.

Drain the spaghetti and place on a serving dish. Pour the sauce over and serve immediately.

◾ COOK'S TIP

When fresh tomatoes are cheap and plentiful, use 150 g/1 lb peeled and chopped fresh instead of canned tomatoes and 1 tablespoon tomato purée.

◾ MICROWAVE TIP

To cook sauce in microwave: cook onion and garlic in oil for 6 minutes. Add mushrooms, walnuts and watercress, cook 2 minutes. Add cream and cook 3 minutes.

163 TAGLIATELLE ALLA CARBONARA

Preparation time:
10-15 minutes

Cooking time:
20-25 minutes

Serves 4

Calories:
700 per portion

YOU WILL NEED:
450 g/1 lb tagliatelle
salt and pepper
100 g/4 oz smoked rindless bacon,
  diced
2 tablespoons oil or 25 g/1 oz butter
2 eggs, lightly beaten
150 ml/¼ pint single cream
2 tablespoons chopped parsley
50 g/2 oz Parmesan cheese, grated

Cook the tagliatelle in a large saucepan of boiling salted water for 10-12 minutes until just tender. Drain and place in a serving dish. Keep warm.

Fry the bacon in the oil or butter until crispy, reduce the heat, then add the eggs, cream, parsley, seasoning to taste and half of the Parmesan. Heat gently, without boiling, stirring. Pour the sauce over the pasta, then sprinkle the remaining Parmesan cheese on top and serve immediately.

164 TAGLIATELLE WITH BLUE CHEESE SAUCE

Preparation time:
5 minutes

Cooking time:
15-20 minutes

Serves 4

Calories:
665 per portion

YOU WILL NEED:
450 g/1 lb green tagliatelle
salt and pepper
300 ml/½ pint single cream
100 g/4 oz Danish Blue cheese
50 g/2 oz chopped walnuts

Cook the tagliatelle in a large saucepan of boiling salted water for 10-12 minutes until just tender. Drain and place in a serving dish. Keep warm. In a saucepan, over a very low heat, heat the cream. Crumble the Danish Blue with your fingers and add to the cream. Add the chopped walnuts and season well.

Heat until the cheese has melted and the sauce is hot – do not let the sauce boil or it will curdle. Pour the sauce over the tagliatelle and serve immediately.

■ COOK'S TIP

For a really quick and easy pasta dish, stir 100 g/4 oz cream cheese with garlic and herbs into the hot drained pasta.

■ COOK'S TIP

Fresh, chilled pasta is available from many supermarkets and delicatessens. Cook for 3-5 minutes according to type.

165 QUICK RAVIOLI SUPPER

Preparation time:
10 minutes

Cooking time:
15-20 minutes

Serves 4

Calories:
285 per portion

YOU WILL NEED:
1 onion, chopped
2 garlic cloves, crushed
1 tablespoon oil
2 × 440 g/15½ oz cans ravioli in
 tomato sauce
50 g/2 oz Cheddar cheese, grated
50 g/2 oz fresh white breadcrumbs

Fry the onion and garlic in the oil for a few minutes until the onion is soft and transparent. Add the ravioli and heat gently for 5 minutes. Pour the mixture into a serving dish, then sprinkle over the Cheddar and breadcrumbs and cook under a hot grill until brown.

Serve immediately with a green salad.

166 PORK CHOW MEIN

Preparation time:
20-25 minutes

Cooking time:
20-25 minutes

Serves 4

Calories:
345 per portion

YOU WILL NEED:
225 g/8 oz Chinese egg noodles
salt and pepper
2 tablespoons oil
225 g/8 oz boneles pork, diced
75 g/3 oz spring onions, chopped
2 garlic cloves, crushed
100 g/4 oz button mushrooms
1 tablespoon soy sauce
2 spring onion curls, to garnish

Cook the noodles in a saucepan of boiling salted water for 5-10 minutes until just tender. Drain well and set aside.

Heat the oil in a large frying pan or wok, and fry the pork for 5 minutes. Add the onion, garlic and mushrooms and continue cooking for 2-3 minutes, then add the noodles, seasoning to taste and soy sauce. Mix all the ingredients together well and cook for 5 minutes or until the noodles are crispy. Serve immediately, garnished as illustrated.

■ COOK'S TIP

Spaghetti in tomato sauce or other shapes of canned pasta can be used in this dish.

■ COOK'S TIP

For chicken chow mein use boneless shredded chicken in place of pork.

167 STUFFED PASTA SHELLS

Preparation time:
15 minutes, plus
time to cool the
pasta

Cooking time:
10-12 minutes

Serves 4

Calories:
525 per portion

YOU WILL NEED:
1 avocado, peeled and diced
1 tablespoon lemon juice
1 × 198 g/7 oz can tuna, drained and
flaked
100 g/4 oz cottage cheese
1 onion, chopped
1 green pepper, seeded and chopped
2 tablespoons mayonnaise
salt and pepper
225 g/8 oz large pasta shells
crisp lettuce, to serve

Brush or dip the avocado in the lemon juice, then mix with the tuna, cottage cheese, onion, pepper and mayonnaise in a bowl, and season well.

Cook the pasta shells in a large saucepan of boiling salted water for 10-12 minutes until just tender. Drain and leave to cool. Stuff the shells with the filling and serve on a bed of crisp lettuce. This dish can be served either as a starter or a light lunch.

168 PASTA SALAD

Preparation time:
15 minutes, plus
time to cool the
pasta

Cooking time:
10-12 minutes

Serves 4

Calories:
495 per portion

YOU WILL NEED:
225 g/8 oz pasta bows
salt and pepper
bunch of spring onions, chopped
1 red pepper, seeded and chopped
1 green pepper, seeded and chopped
2 celery sticks, sliced
1 tablespoon chopped parsley
150 ml/¼ pint natural yogurt
150 ml/¼ pint mayonnaise
1 teaspoon honey
¼ teaspoon freshly grated nutmeg

Cook the pasta bows in a large saucepan of boiling salted water for 10-12 minutes until just tender. Drain and leave to cool.

In a large mixing bowl, combine all the salad ingredients. Add the pasta. Mix together the yogurt, mayonnaise, honey and nutmeg. Transfer the salad to a serving bowl, and pour over the dressing. Serve with crisp lettuce leaves.

▨ COOK'S TIP

These stuffed pasta shells can be served individually as a tasty first course, with a light tomato dressing. Stir 1 tablespoon tomato purée and a generous dash of
Worcestershire sauce into 150 ml/¼ pint soured cream. Season with garlic salt and pepper. Spoon this dressing over the pasta shells.

▨ COOK'S TIP

Add cooked or canned fish or meat to this salad for a more substantial lunch or supper dish. If adding fish use small pasta shells instead of bows.

PIES, FLANS & PASTIES

A pie or flan will suit almost any occasion, from the simple to the sumptuous, depending on how extravagant you are with the filling ingredients. This chapter has recipes using lots of different kinds of pastry from puff and choux to suet and shortcrust.

169 SAUSAGE LAYER PIE

Preparation time:
20 minutes

Cooking time:
1 hour

Oven temperature:
190 C, 375 F, gas 5

Serves 4

Calories:
905 per portion

YOU WILL NEED:
1 × recipe shortcrust pastry (recipe 176)
beaten egg, to glaze
FOR THE FILLING
350 g/12 oz sausagemeat
1 onion, chopped
2 garlic cloves, crushed
100 g/4 oz fresh breadcrumbs
salt and pepper
75 g/3 oz stuffed green olives
3 peperoni sausages

Make the shortcrust pastry as instructed in recipe 176. Roll out two-thirds of the pastry to line a 450 g/1 lb loaf tin.

Combine the sausagemeat, onion, garlic, breadcrumbs and seasoning. Spoon a little into the base of the tin, smooth over and top with a layer of olives and peperoni sausage. Repeat the layers until all the ingredients are used up, finishing with the sausagemeat mixture. Roll out the remaining pastry to form a lid. Dampen the edge of the pastry with water and cover the pie with the pastry lid. Trim and seal the edges and make a small hole in the centre to allow any steam to escape. Use any pastry trimmings to make leaves to garnish the top of the pie. Glaze with beaten egg and cook in a moderately hot oven for about 1 hour. Serve hot or cold with a salad.

■ COOK'S TIP

Peel, core and slice cooking apples to layer in the sausagemeat pie.

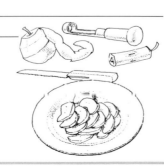

170 STEAK AND KIDNEY PUDDING

Preparation time:
20 minutes

Cooking time:
4 hours

Serves 4

Calories:
640 per portion

YOU WILL NEED:
225 g/8 oz self-raising flour
salt and pepper
100 g/4 oz shredded suet
6-8 tablespoons cold water, plus
    150 ml/¼ pint
450 g/1 lb stewing steak
100 g/4 oz kidney
1 onion, chopped
25 g/1 oz plain flour
pinch of mustard powder

Sift the flour and ½ teaspoon salt into a bowl. Add the suet and mix well, then stir in sufficient water to form a light, elastic dough. Roll out two-thirds of the pastry to a circle large enough to line a 900 ml/1½ pint pudding basin.

Cut the steak into 2.5 cm/1 inch cubes. Remove skin, core and fat from the kidney, then cut into 1 cm/½ inch pieces. Arrange the steak and kidney in layers in the pudding basin. Mix together the onion, flour, mustard, seasoning to taste and the 150 ml/¼ pint water until smooth. Pour over the meat.

Roll out the remaining pastry to form a circle to fit the top of the basin. Brush the rim of the pudding with water, lift the pastry lid over the basin and press down gently around the rim. Trim off surplus pastry.

Cover with a lid of greaseproof paper, then a lid of foil, both pleated to allow for expansion, and tie with string. Steam or boil the pudding for 4 hours, topping up with boiling water as required.

■ COOK'S TIP

Traditionally ox kidney is used in this recipe, but if you prefer a milder flavour use lamb's kidneys.

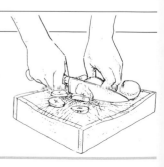

171 SPICY MEAT PIES

Preparation time:
25 minutes

Cooking time:
45-50 minutes

Oven temperature:
200 C, 400 F, gas 6

Makes 24

Calories:
130 per portion

YOU WILL NEED:
1 onion, chopped
1 garlic clove, crushed
1 green pepper, seeded and chopped
1 tablespoon oil
225 g/8 oz minced beef
½ teaspoon chilli powder
1 teaspoon Worcestershire sauce
2 tablespoons tomato ketchup
150 ml/¼ pint beef stock
2 teaspoons plain flour
1-2 tablespoons water
salt and pepper
1½ × recipe shortcrust pastry (recipe 176)
beaten egg, to glaze

Fry the vegetables in the oil until soft. Add the beef and cook gently 5 minutes. Stir in the chilli powder, Worcestershire sauce, ketchup and stock, and simmer gently 15 minutes. Mix the flour to a paste with a little cold water, add to the pan and simmer 5 minutes. Season and let cool.

Make the shortcrust pastry as instructed in recipe 176. Roll out thinly, then, using a floured tartlet cutter, stamp out 24 rounds. Use a slightly smaller cutter to stamp out 24 lids. Place the larger rounds into lightly greased tartlet tins and put a spoonful of the mince mixture in each. Dampen the edges of the pastry with a little water and cover each one with a pastry lid. Seal the edges, brush with beaten egg and bake in a moderately hot oven for about 20 minutes.

■ COOK'S TIP

A quick way of making shortcrust: chill the fat in the freezer, dip in the flour, then grate coarsely. Mix into flour with enough water to bind.

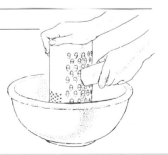

172 CORNISH PASTIES

Preparation time:
20 minutes

Cooking time:
1 hour

Oven temperature:
190 C, 375 F, gas 5

Serves 4

Calories:
510 per pasty

YOU WILL NEED:
1 × recipe shortcrust pastry (recipe 176)
beaten egg, to glaze
FOR THE FILLING
225 g/8 oz braising steak
1 potato
1 onion
225 g/8 oz swede
2 tablespoons beef stock
salt and pepper

Make the shortcrust pastry as instructed in recipe 176 and chill while preparing the filling. Cut the meat and potato into small cubes. Chop the onion and swede. Mix the meat and vegetables with the stock and season generously.

Grease a baking tray. Divide the pastry into four pieces and roll each piece out to a 15 cm 6 inch circle. Divide the meat mixture between the pastry circles and dampen the edges with water. Bring the edges together over the middle of the filling and seal, making a fluted pattern with your fingertips, to form an enclosed pasty.

Place on the baking tray and brush with beaten egg. Bake in a moderately hot oven for 1 hour. Serve hot or cold, with a salad and pickles.

■ COOK'S TIP

For economy, substitute minced beef for the braising steak. Carrots or turnips can be used instead of swedes.

173 PIZZA

Preparation time:
20 minutes

Cooking time:
25 minutes

Oven temperature:
230 C, 450 F, gas 8

Serves 2

Calories:
730 per portion

YOU WILL NEED:
1 × 141 g/5 oz packet bread or pizza
 mix
1 onion, sliced into rings
1 garlic clove, crushed
50 g/2 oz mushrooms, sliced
25 g/1 oz butter or margarine
4 tomatoes, peeled
1 × 190 g/6¾ oz can pimientos
50 g/2 oz salami
100 g/4 oz mozzarella cheese, diced
pinch of oregano
salt and pepper
6-8 black olives
chopped parsley, to garnish

Make the dough base as instructed on the packet. Press or roll out to a 20 cm/8 inch round on a baking tray and leave to rise for 5 minutes.

Meanwhile cook the onion, garlic and mushrooms in the butter or margarine for a few minutes. Cut the tomatoes into eighths. Drain the pimientos and cut into strips. Thinly slice the salami.

Place the tomatoes and onion mixture on the pizza base, leaving a 5 mm/¼ inch border all round. Arrange the pimientos and salami on top, then sprinkle over the mozzarella, oregano, seasoning and olives. Bake in a hot oven for 20 minutes and sprinkle with parsley to serve.

174 CHICKEN PIE

Preparation time:
25 minutes

Cooking time:
2 hours 50 minutes

Oven temperature:
190 C, 375 F, gas 5

Serves 4

Calories:
675 per portion

YOU WILL NEED:
1 small boiling chicken
2 onions
salt and pepper
225 g/8 oz mushrooms
25 g/1 oz butter
1 × 298g/10½ oz can condensed
 mushroom soup
1 tablespoon lemon juice
½ teaspoon tarragon
1 × 368 g/13 oz packet frozen puff
 pastry, defrosted
beaten egg, to glaze

Place the chicken with one onion and seasoning in a large pan. Cover with water. Bring to the boil and simmer for about 2½ hours, or until tender. Drain and reserve the liquid for chicken stock.

Chop the remaining onion and slice the mushrooms. Cook the vegetables in the butter for a few minutes. Dice the chicken meat. Mix together the filling ingredients with 150 ml/¼ pint of the reserved stock and season to taste. Pour into an oval dish.

Roll out the pastry to 5 mm/¼ in thick. Dampen the rim of the pie dish and cover with a strip of pastry. Brush the strip with water and cover with the remaining pastry to make a lid. Press the edges together, knock up and flute. Brush with beaten egg and decorate with any pastry trimmings made into leaves. Glaze the decorations and bake in a moderately hot oven for 35-40 minutes.

■ FREEZER TIP

Bake several pizza bases without topping. Remove from oven when three-quarters cooked, cool and freeze. Grill base, turn and add topping, then grill top.

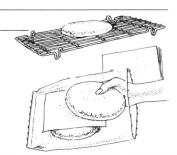

■ COOK'S TIP

Knock up the edges of pies to seal the join. Press the edge of the pastry outwards, while knocking it inwards with the blunt edge of a knife at a slight angle.

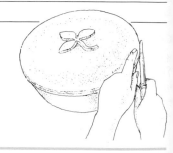

175 VEGETABLE PIE

Preparation time:
25 minutes

Cooking time:
45-55 minutes

Oven temperature:
190 C, 375 F, gas 5

Serves 4

Calories:
540 per portion

YOU WILL NEED:
1 × recipe wholemeal pastry (recipe 185)
beaten egg, to glaze
FOR THE FILLING
225 g/8 oz broccoli
2 celery sticks
2 leeks, trimmed
2 carrots
2 parsnips
1 red pepper, seeded
1 tablespoon lemon juice
¼ teaspoon grated nutmeg
salt and pepper
1 × recipe white sauce (recipe 156), using 40 g/1½ oz each fat and flour

Make the wholemeal pastry as instructed in recipe 185 and refrigerate. Break the broccoli into sprigs. Cut the celery into chunks and slice the leeks into rings. Slice the carrots and parsnips. Cut the pepper into strips. Arrange the vegetables in a deep oval pie dish. Add the lemon juice, nutmeg and seasoning to the white sauce and pour over the vegetables.

Roll out the pastry to 5 mm/¼ in thick, dampen the rim of the pie dish and cover with a strip of pastry cut from the outside of the oval. Brush the strip with water and cover the pie with the remaining pastry. Press the edges together, knock up and flute. Brush with beaten egg and decorate the pie with any pastry trimmings made into leaves. Glaze the decorations and bake in a moderately hot oven for 40-50 minutes.

■ COOK'S TIP

Cheese pastry tastes good with vegetable pie. Stir 50 g/2 oz finely grated mature Cheddar chese into the dry ingredients. Continue as above.

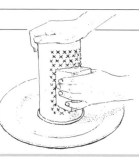

176 PORK PARCELS

Preparation time:
25 minutes

Cooking time:
1 hour 5 minutes

Oven temperature:
180 C, 350 F, gas 4

Serves 4

Calories:
635 per portion

YOU WILL NEED:
350 g/12 oz lean pork
1 onion, chopped
1 tablespoon oil
100 g/4 oz no-need-to-soak dried apricots
2 tablespoons orange juice
salt and pepper
FOR THE SHORTCRUST PASTRY
225 g/8 oz plain flour
pinch of salt
100 g/4 oz margarine
2-3 tablespoons cold water
beaten egg, to glaze

Cut the pork into small cubes and mix with the onion; fry in the oil for a few minutes. Roughly chop the apricots, add to the pork with the orange juice and seasoning.

Sift the flour and salt into a bowl. Cut the margarine into small pieces and rub into the flour until the mixture resembles fine breadcrumbs. Add enough water to mix to a soft dough.

Divide the pastry into four pieces and roll each piece out to a 15 cm/6 inch circle. Divide the pork mixture between the rounds, dampen the edges with water and bring together to one side of the filling. Seal and pinch the edges and place the parcels on a greased baking tray. Brush with beaten egg and bake in a moderate oven for 1 hour. Garnish as illustrated and serve with a salad.

■ COOK'S TIP

If you do not have a rolling pin use a clean empty wine bottle to roll out.

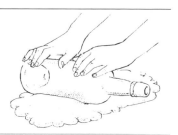

177 CRUNCHY FISH PIE

Preparation time:
15-20 minutes

Cooking time:
35-45 minutes

Oven temperature:
190 C, 375 F, gas 5

Serves 4

Calories:
725 per portion

YOU WILL NEED:
50 g/2 oz butter or margarine
50 g/2 oz plain flour
600 ml/1 pint milk
salt and pepper
¼ teaspoon dill weed
*1 × 198g/7 oz can tuna, drained and
    flaked*
100 g/4 oz peeled cooked prawns
2 tablespoons lemon juice
FOR THE TOPPING
175 g/6 oz wholemeal flour
50 g/2 oz oatmeal
100 g/4 oz butter
salt and pepper
FOR THE GARNISH
2 whole cooked prawns
parsley sprigs

Melt the butter or margarine over a low heat, stir in the flour, cook for 2 minutes, then gradually add the milk, stirring all the time. Bring the sauce to the boil, simmer gently for a few minutes. Add the seasoning, dill weed, tuna, prawns and lemon juice. Pour into an ovenproof dish.

Place the flour, oatmeal, butter and seasoning in a bowl. Using your fingertips, rub the fat into the dry ingredients until the mixture resembles fine breadcrumbs. Spoon over the fish mixture and bake in a moderately hot oven for 30-40 minutes. Serve hot, garnished with whole prawns and parsley.

178 FISH ENVELOPES

Preparation time:
15 minutes

Cooking time:
20-25 minutes

Oven temperature:
220 C, 425 F, gas 7

Serves 4

Calories:
585 per envelope

YOU WILL NEED:
*450 g/1 lb smoked haddock, skinned
    and boned*
1 large onion, chopped
50 g/2 oz butter or margarine
2 hard-boiled eggs, chopped
2 tablespoons chopped parsley
2 tablespoons natural yogurt
salt and pepper
*1 × 368 g/13 oz packet frozen puff
    pastry, defrosted*
beaten egg, to glaze
FOR THE GARNISH
watercress sprigs
tomato lily

Grease two baking trays. Cut the fish into small pieces and cook with the onion in the butter or margarine for 5 minutes. Mix the hard-boiled eggs, parsley, yogurt and seasoning with the fish and onion. Leave to cool while preparing the pastry envelopes.

Divide the pastry into four and roll into 18 cm/7 inch squares. Divide the fish mixture between the squares, keeping it well in the centre. Dampen the edges of the pastry with a little water and bring the four corners to the centre, pressing well together to seal. Glaze the pastry envelopes with beaten egg, transfer to the baking trays and bake in a hot oven for 15-20 minutes, until golden. Serve immediately, garnished with watercress and a tomato lily.

■ MICROWAVE TIP

Whisk butter, flour and milk and microwave on full power 8-10 minutes. Whisk, add seafood, microwave 3-5 minutes, transfer to serving dish, top and grill.

■ MICROWAVE TIP

Defrost frozen puff pastry in the microwave. Unwrap and place on double thick absorbent kitchen paper. Allow 1 minute on full power, turning once.

179 KIPPER FLAN

Preparation time:
20-25 minutes

Cooking time:
35 minutes

Oven temperature:
180 C, 350 F, gas 4

Serves 4

Calories:
570 per portion

YOU WILL NEED:
¾ × recipe shortcrust pastry (recipe 176)
FOR THE FILLING
225 g/8 oz kipper fillets
40 g/1½ oz butter or margarine
40 g/1½ oz plain flour
450 ml/¾ pint milk
2 tablespoons lemon juice
2 hard-boiled eggs, chopped
½ teaspoon dried sage
salt and pepper
FOR THE GARNISH
parsley sprigs
tomato wedges

Make the shortcrust pastry as instructed in recipe 176, using wholemeal flour if you prefer. Roll out on a lightly floured board to line a 20 cm/8 inch flan dish or ring. Bake blind in a moderate oven for 15-20 minutes (see Cook's Tip below).

Meanwhile, simmer the kipper fillets in boiling water for 7-10 minutes. Drain and flake. Melt the butter or margarine over a low heat, add the flour and cook for 2 minutes, stirring continuously, then gradually add the milk, stirring, until the sauce boils and thickens. Reduce the heat and simmer for a few minutes, then add the flaked fish, lemon juice, chopped eggs, sage and seasoning. Pour into the pastry case and bake in the oven for a further 10 minutes. Serve hot, garnished with parsley and tomato.

180 RICH SALAMI FLAN

Preparation time:
20 minutes

Cooking time:
35-40 minutes

Oven temperature:
180 C, 350 F, gas 4

Serves 4

Calories:
610 per portion

YOU WILL NEED:
¾ × recipe shortcrust pastry (recipe 176)
FOR THE FILLING
1 onion
1 red pepper, seeded
100 g/4 oz salami, thinly sliced
50 g/2 oz Cheddar cheese, grated
2 eggs
150 ml/¼ pint milk
150 ml/¼ pint single cream
salt and pepper
FOR THE GARNISH
3-4 stuffed green olives
parsley sprigs

Make the shortcrust pastry as instructed in recipe 176. Roll out on a lightly floured board and use to line a 20 cm/8 inch flan dish or ring.

Finely chop the onion and pepper, spread over the pastry base. Arrange the salami slices on top, reserving a few for garnish, and sprinkle over the Cheddar. Lightly beat together the eggs, milk, cream and seasoning and pour over the salami mixture.

Bake in a moderate oven for 35-40 minutes, until golden. Garnish with the remainig salami slices, rolled into cones, the olives and parsley. Serve hot or cold with a mushroom and tomato salad.

■ COOK'S TIP

To bake blind, place a sheet of greaseproof paper in the pastry case. Sprinkle in baking beans or dried peas. Bake as directed, then remove the peas and paper.

■ COOK'S TIP

Use a pastry blender to rub the fat into the flour. Cut the fat into pieces, then use the blender with a bouncing action, mixing the flour and fat.

181 ONION FLAN

Preparation time: 20 minutes	YOU WILL NEED: *¾ × recipe shortcrust pastry (recipe 176)*
Cooking time: 35-40 minutes	FOR THE FILLING *450 g/1 lb onions, chopped*
Oven temperature: 180 C, 350 F, gas 4	*50 g/2 oz margarine* *50 g/2 oz fresh white breadcrumbs*
Serves 4	*100 g/4 oz Cheddar cheese, grated* *2 eggs*
Calories: 620 per portion	*300 ml/½ pint milk* *salt and pepper* *paprika, to sprinkle* *onion rings, to garnish*

Make the shortcrust pastry as instructed in recipe 176 and roll out to line a 20 cm/8 inch flan dish.

Cook the onion in the fat until softened and transparent. Cool slightly. Spoon the onions and breadcrumbs into the flan case, sprinkle over the Cheddar. Lightly beat the eggs, milk and seasoning together, pour over the cheese mixture. Sprinkle with paprika and bake in a moderate oven for 35-40 minutes. Serve hot, garnished with a few raw onion rings.

182 QUICHE LORRAINE

Preparation time: 25-30 minutes	YOU WILL NEED: *¾ × recipe shortcrust pastry (recipe 176)*
Cooking time: 40-45 minutes	FOR THE FILLING *1 onion, chopped*
Oven temperature: 190 C, 375 F, gas 5	*4 rashers rindless streaky bacon, diced* *1 tablespoon oil*
Serves 4	*100 g/4 oz Cheddar cheese, grated* *2 eggs*
Calories: 590 per portion	*300 ml/½ pint milk* *salt and pepper* *paprika, to sprinkle*

Make the shortcrust pastry as instructed in recipe 176. Roll out on a lightly floured board to line a 20 cm/8 inch fluted flan ring placed on a baking tray.

Fry the onion and bacon in the oil for a few minutes, cool slightly, then spread evenly over the pastry. Sprinkle half the Cheddar over the bacon mixture. Beat the eggs, milk and seasoning together and pour into the flan case. Sprinkle the remaining cheese on top and dust with paprika. Bake in a moderately hot oven for 40-45 minutes. Serve hot or cold with a mixed salad.

■ COOK'S TIP

For a satisfactory starter make individual flans and serve freshly cooked.

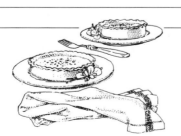

■ COOK'S TIP

Scissors can be used to dice bacon. First cut the rashers lengthways into thin strips. Holding the strips together snip them across into small pieces.

183 SWEETCORN FLAN

Preparation time:
20 25 minutes

Cooking time:
25 minutes

Oven temperature:
190 C, 375 F, gas 5

Serves 4

Calories:
510 per portion

YOU WILL NEED:
¾ × recipe shortcrust pastry (recipe 176)
FOR THE FILLING
1 onion, chopped
1 green pepper, seeded and chopped
1 tablespoon oil
1 × 326 g/11½ oz can sweetcorn
100 g/4 oz cooked ham, diced
40 g/1½ oz butter or margarine
40 g/1½ oz plain flour
450 ml/¾ pint milk
salt and pepper
FOR THE GARNISH
3 tomatoes, sliced
parsley sprig

Make the shortcrust pastry as instructed in recipe 176. Roll out and line a 20 cm/8 inch flan ring placed on a baking tray. Bake blind (see Cook's Tip 179) for 15 minutes in a moderately hot oven, then remove the paper and beans and return to the oven for a further 10 minutes.

Meanwhile, cook the onion and pepper in the oil for a few minutes until soft. Drain the sweetcorn and add to the mixture with the ham.

Make a white sauce using the butter or margarine, flour and milk as instructed in recipe 156. Add the vegetable mixture and simmer gently for 2 minutes. Season well.

Pour the mixture into the cooked warm flan case, garnish with halved tomato slices and parsley and serve.

184 RATATOUILLE QUICHE

Preparation time:
30 minutes

Cooking time:
35-40 minutes

Oven temperature:
190 C, 375 F, gas 5

Serves 4

Calories:
560 per portion

YOU WILL NEED:
¾ × recipe shortcrust pastry (recipe 176)
FOR THE FILLING
1 red pepper, seeded and cut into rings
1 green pepper, seeded and cut into rings
1 onion, diced
1 garlic clove, crushed
2 small courgettes, sliced
2 tomatoes, peeled and quartered
50 g/2 oz butter or margarine
3 eggs
300 ml/½ pint milk
salt and pepper
50 g/2 oz Cheddar cheese, grated
chopped parsley, to garnish

Make the shortcrust pastry as instructed in recipe 176. Roll out on a lightly floured board and use to line a 20 cm/8 inch flan dish or ring placed on a baking tray.

Cook the vegetables in the butter or margarine until soft, arrange in the pastry case. Lightly beat the eggs with the milk and seasoning, pour over the vegetables and sprinkle with the Cheddar. Bake in a moderately hot oven for 35-40 minutes. Garnish with chopped parsley and serve hot with green beans and new potatoes.

COOK'S TIP

Quick flan case: melt 100 g/4 oz margarine, stir in 175 g/6 oz crushed savoury biscuits. Press in the base and sides of the dish. Chill, fill and serve.

COOK'S TIP

Flavour the pastry with 2 tablespoons oregano for this flan.

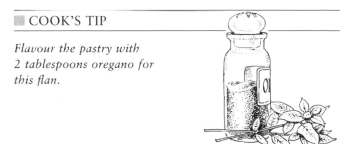

185 BROCCOLI QUICHE

Preparation time:	YOU WILL NEED:
20 minutes	FOR THE WHOLEMEAL PASTRY
	225 g/8 oz plain wholemeal flour
Cooking time:	pinch of salt
40-45 minutes	pinch of paprika
	100 g/4 oz margarine
Oven temperature:	2-3 tablespoons cold water
190 C, 375 F, gas 5	FOR THE FILLING
	225 g/8 oz broccoli
Serves 4	2 eggs
Calories:	300 ml/½ pint milk
585 per portion	salt and pepper
	100 g/4 oz Cheddar cheese, grated

Sift the flour, salt and paprika into a bowl. Cut the margarine into small pieces and rub into the flour until the mixture resembles breadcrumbs. Add enough water to mix to a soft dough. Roll out on a lightly floured surface and use to line a 20 cm/8 inch flan dish or ring placed on a baking tray.

Blanch the broccoli in boiling water for 2-3 minutes. Drain very well and cut into neat chunks. Arrange in the flan case. Beat the eggs, milk and seasoning together, pour over the broccoli. Sprinkle with the grated Cheddar.

Bake in a moderately hot oven for 35-40 minutes or until set. Serve hot, with sautéed potatoes.

186 COURGETTE QUICHE

Preparation time:	YOU WILL NEED:
25-30 minutes	1 × recipe wholemeal pastry (recipe 185)
Cooking time:	FOR THE FILLING
40-45 minutes	450 g/1 lb courgettes, sliced
	1 garlic clove, crushed
Oven temperature:	1 onion, chopped
190 C, 375 F, gas 5	1 tablespoon oil
	100 g/4 oz Cheddar cheese, grated
Serves 4	2 eggs
Calories:	300 ml/½ pint milk
615 per portion	salt and pepper
	FOR THE GARNISH
	tomato slices
	cress

Make the wholemeal pastry as instructed in recipe 185. Roll out on a lightly floured surface and use to line a 20 cm/8 inch flan dish or ring placed on a baking tray.

Cook the courgettes, garlic and onion in the oil until softened. Arrange in the pastry case and sprinkle over the grated Cheddar. Lightly beat the eggs, milk and seasoning together, pour over the cheese mixture.

Bake in a moderately hot oven for 35-40 minutes. Garnish with tomato and cress and accompany with a coleslaw salad.

◾ MICROWAVE TIP

Instead of blanching the broccoli put it in a roasting bag with 2 tablespoons water and microwave on high 3-4 minutes. Snip the corner off the bag and drain.

◾ COOK'S TIP

To lift pastry into a flan tin, fold it over the rolling pin, then lift it loosely over the tin. Press in with fingertips.

187 SAMOSAS

Preparation time:
10-25 minutes

Cooking time:
25-30 minutes

Makes 10

Calories:
155 per samosa

YOU WILL NEED:

225 g/8 oz minced beef or lamb
1 onion, finely chopped
1 small pepper, seeded and finely
   chopped
1 small carrot, diced
1 small potato, diced
2 garlic cloves, crushed
1½ tablespoons garam masala
salt and pepper
225 g/8 oz self-raising flour
4 tablespoons oil, plus oil for deep
   frying
1 egg
2 tablespoons water

Cook the meat and onion gently until the fat runs. Add the vegetables and seasoning and simmer for 10 minutes, stirring frequently. Leave to cool.

Sift the flour and a pinch of salt into a bowl. Mix in the 4 tablespoons oil, the egg and water to make a dough. Knead gently on a lightly floured surface until smooth. Divide into ten equal portions and roll out each portion to a 13 cm/5 inch square. Place some of the filling in the middle of each square. Dampen the edges with water, fold one top corner over to the opposite corner and seal the edges to form a triangular pasty. Heat the oil for deep frying and fry the samosas, a few at a time, for about 5 minutes or until golden. Drain on absorbent kitchen paper and keep warm while cooking the remainder. Garnish the samosas as illustrated and serve hot with a cucumber raita. (See Cook's Tip below.)

188 SAUSAGE PLAIT

Preparation time:
10-15 minutes

Cooking time:
40-45 minutes

Oven temperature:
190 C, 375 F, gas 5

Serves 4

Calories:
790 per portion

YOU WILL NEED:

1 × 368 g/13 oz packet frozen puff
   pastry, defrosted
beaten egg, to glaze
FOR THE FILLING
450 g/1 lb sausagemeat
1 onion, finely chopped
1 tablespoon chutney
1 teaspoon dried sage
salt and pepper

Roll out the pastry to an oblong measuring 25cm × 35 cm/10 × 14 inches. Mix all the filling ingredients together, season well. Arrange the filling down the middle of the pastry. Cut the edges of the pastry diagonally into 2.5 cm/1 inch strips, up to the filling. Fold these strips of pastry over the filling to form a plait, dampening the edges with water in order to hold them in place.

Brush with a little beaten egg and bake in a moderately hot oven for 40-45 minutes. Serve hot or cold, with a salad.

■ COOK'S TIP

Grate ¼ cucumber. Put in a sieve, sprinkle with salt and drain. Squeeze out liquid, then mix with 150 ml/¼ pint natural yogurt and 1 teaspoon chopped mint.

■ COOK'S TIP

Add 100 g/4 oz finely diced mature Cheddar cheese to the filling. Continue as above.

189 CHICKEN AND CHEESE PUFFS

Preparation time:
25-30 minutes

Cooking time:
35-40 minutes

Oven temperature:
200 C, 400 F, gas 6

Makes 6

Calories:
410 per puff

YOU WILL NEED:
225 g/8 oz cooked chicken
1 onion
1 red pepper
1 green pepper
100 g/4 oz mushrooms
1 tablespoon oil
100 g/4 oz Cheddar cheese
1 tablespoon chopped parsley
salt and pepper
1 × 368 g/13 oz packet frozen puff
    pastry, defrosted
beaten egg, to glaze

Dice the chicken. Chop the onion and seed and dice the peppers. Slice the mushrooms thinly. Cook the vegetables in the oil for a few minutes. Cool.

Dice the Cheddar. Mix together all the ingredients, add the parsley and season to taste.

Roll out the pastry to a 38 × 25 cm/15 × 10 inch rectangle and cut into six 13 cm/5 inch squares. Spoon the chicken filling into the centre of each, dampen the edges with a little water and fold over to make a triangle. Press the edges well to seal and brush with beaten egg.

Placed on a greased baking tray and bake in a moderately hot oven for 35-40 minutes.

190 VOLS-AU-VENT

Preparation time:
20-25 minutes

Cooking time:
25 minutes

Oven temperature:
220 C, 425 F, gas 7
and
200 C, 400 F, gas 6

Makes 12

Calories:
340 per vol-au-vent

YOU WILL NEED:
2 × 368 g/13 oz packets frozen puff
    pastry, defrosted
beaten egg, to glaze
FOR THE FILLINGS
¾ × recipe white sauce (recipe 156)
50 g/2 oz Cheddar cheese, grated
50 g/2 oz cooked ham, diced
100 g/4 oz peeled cooked prawns
1 tablespoon lemon juice
50 g/2 oz sliced cooked mushrooms
100 g/4 oz cooked chicken, diced
1 tablespoon dry sherry
salt and pepper

Roll out the pastry to 5 mm/¼ inch thickness and stamp out 24 circles using a 7.5 cm/3 inch plain cutter. Transfer 12 circles to a greased baking tray, prick with a fork and brush with beaten egg. Using a 5 cm/2 inch cutter, cut out the centres of the remaining circles. Lift the rings carefully on to the bases, press down firmly. Glaze the cases and bake in a hot oven for 15 minutes, then reduce to moderately hot for a further 10 minutes.

Divide the sauce into three; add the Cheddar and ham to one third, the prawns and lemon juice to another, and the mushrooms, chicken, sherry and seasoning to the final third. Fill the vol-au-vent cases. Reheat in a hot oven before serving, garnishing as illustrated if you like.

■ COOK'S TIP

If you have a non-stick baking tray, there is no need to grease it for puff pastry. Dampen the surface and the steam during cooking will help the pastry puff.

■ COOK'S TIP

To use pastry cutters successfully for clean shapes, have a small patch of flour near and dip the cutter in it each time it is used.

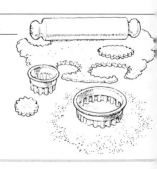

191 SAVOURY PUFFS

Preparation time:
20 minutes

Cooking time:
25-30 minutes

Oven temperature:
220 C, 425 F, gas 7

Makes 24

Calories:
100 per puff

YOU WILL NEED:
½ × recipe choux pastry (recipe 192)
paprika to sprinkle
FOR THE FILLING
50 g/2 oz butter or margarine
50 g/2 oz plain flour
300 ml/½ pint milk
150 ml/¼ pint dry white wine
100 g/4 oz blue cheese
50 g/2 oz chopped walnuts
1 tablespoon lemon juice
1 tablespoon chopped parsley
salt and pepper

Make the choux pastry as instructed in recipe 192, omitting the grated cheese. Spoon or pipe 24 small puffs on to a greased baking tray. Bake in a hot oven for 20-25 minutes, then cool on a wire rack. Make a slit in each bun immediately they are removed from the oven to allow any steam to escape.

To make the filling, melt the butter or margarine over a low heat, stir in the flour, then gradually add the milk and wine, stirring continuously. Bring the sauce to the boil, simmer gently for a few minutes. Remove from the heat and crumble in the blue cheese with the walnuts, lemon juice, parsley and seasoning. Using a teaspoon, fill the buns with the sauce. Sprinkle with paprika and serve hot, either as a starter or to have with drinks.

192 GOUGERE

Preparation time:
20 minutes

Cooking time:
50 minutes

Oven temperature:
200 C, 400 F, gas 6

Serves 4

Calories:
780 per portion

YOU WILL NEED:
FOR THE CHOUX PASTRY
300 ml/½ pint water
100 g/4 oz butter or margarine
175 g/6 oz plain flour
pinch of salt
4 eggs lightly beaten
50 g/2 oz Gruyère cheese, grated
FOR THE FILLING
1 × recipe white sauce (recipe 156)
225 g/8 oz cooked chicken, diced
3 tablespoons lemon juice
pinch of mustard powder
2 teaspoons tarragon
salt and pepper

Place the water in a pan with the fat, heat gently until melted, then bring to the boil. Remove from the heat, add the flour and salt and beat quickly to form a smooth paste which comes away from the sides of the pan to form a ball. Cool slightly, then gradually beat in the eggs to give a smooth glossy mixture. Fold in the grated Gruyère. Spoon or pipe the mixture around the sides of a buttered oval ovenproof dish.

Mix together all the filling ingredients and simmer gently for 5 minutes. Pour into the centre of the dish and bake in a moderately hot oven for 40 minutes. Serve the gougère hot, sprinkled with paprika.

COOK'S TIP

To spoon choux pastry on to a tray, use two teaspoons. Scrape the pastry from spoon to spoon about twice to make even-shaped buns.

FREEZER TIP

Line the baking dish with foil and grease well. Pipe the pastry round the edge, then bake empty. Cool, lift out foil and freeze.

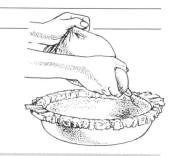

HOT PUDDINGS

Apple charlotte, rhubarb crumble, treacle tart – however figure conscious we are it is hard to resist a pudding for 'afters'. Here you will find all your traditional favourites as well as some new and different ideas. So even if you don't eat puddings every day there is lots of choice for a weekend treat.

193 CITRUS QUEEN OF PUDDINGS

Preparation time:
30 minutes

Cooking time:
50 minutes

Oven temperature:
180 C, 350 F, gas 4

Serves 4

Calories:
380 per portion

YOU WILL NEED:
300 ml/½ pint milk
25 g/1 oz butter
150 g/5 oz caster sugar
100 g/4 oz fresh white breadcrumbs
grated rind and juice of 1 orange
2 eggs, separated
2 tablespoons lemon curd
FOR THE DECORATION
angelica
lemon slices

Gently heat the milk, butter and 25 g/1 oz of the sugar together until the sugar has dissolved. Remove from the heat, add the breadcrumbs and orange rind and juice. Leave the mixture to cool. Beat in the egg yolks. Pour the custard mixture into a 1.2 litre/2 pint buttered pie dish and bake in a moderate oven for 30 minutes.

Spread the lemon curd evenly over the top of the cooked custard. Whisk the egg whites until they stand in stiff peaks, then gradually whisk in the remaining sugar. Carefully spoon or pipe the meringue mixture over the custard. Bake for a further 15 minutes or until the meringue is set and golden. Decorate with angelica and lemon slices cut into eighths.

194 CHRISTMAS PUDDING

Preparation time:
20 minutes, plus at least 2 months storage for maturing

Cooking time:
8-8½ hours

Serves 8

Calories:
530 per portion

YOU WILL NEED:
175 g/6 oz currants
175 g/6 oz raisins
175 g/6 oz sultanas
175 g/6 oz shredded suet
100 g/4 oz fresh white breadcrumbs
100 g/4 oz plain flour
100 g/4 oz demerara sugar
25 g/1 oz glacé cherries, chopped
25 g/1 oz chopped mixed peel
1 teaspoon grated lemon rind
½ teaspoon mixed spice
½ teaspoon nutmeg
¼ teaspoon salt
1 tablespoon black treacle
2 eggs, lightly beaten
150 ml/¼ pint brown ale
4 tablespoons brandy

Grease and line a 1 litre/2 pint pudding basin. In a large bowl, mix all the ingredients using a wooden spoon. Place in the pudding basin and top with a circle of greaseproof paper. Cover with greaseproof paper and a piece of greased cooking foil, pleated to allow for expansion. Secure with string. Steam the pudding in a saucepan half-full of water for 6 hours, topping up with boiling water if necessary. Cool, then store in a dry place for at least two months.

To serve, steam as above for a further 2-2½ hours, then turn out on to a serving plate. Decorate as illustrated with lightly whipped cream and a sprig of holly.

■ COOK'S TIP

To fill a large piping bag, put it in a large jug and fold the open end over the rim of the jug. Spoon in the meringue.

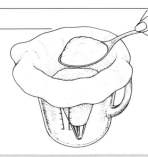

■ COOK'S TIP

To flame the pudding, warm 3 tablespoons brandy, pour over the pudding, light, and carry to the table immediately.

195 CHOCOLATE PUDDING

Preparation time:
20 minutes

Cooking time:
1½ hours

Serves 4

Calories:
715 per portion

YOU WILL NEED:
100 g/4 oz soft margarine
100 g/4 oz caster sugar
2 eggs, lightly beaten
25 g/1 oz cocoa powder
100 g/4 oz self-raising flour
50 g/2 oz plain chocolate, grated
FOR THE MOCHA SAUCE
25 g/1 oz butter
25 g/1 oz plain flour
600 ml/1 pint milk
50 g/2 oz caster sugar
1 tablespoon cocoa powder
1 tablespoon instant coffee

Grease a 1 litre/2 pint pudding basin.

Beat the margarine and sugar until soft and creamy, then gradually beat in the eggs. Fold in the sifted cocoa, flour and chocolate. Pour the mixture into the prepared basin and cover with greased greaseproof paper and a piece of greased cooking foil, pleated to allow for rising. Secure with string. Steam on a trivet or upturned saucer in a saucepan half-full of water for 1½ hours.

To make the sauce, melt the butter over a low heat, add the flour and, stirring continuously, cook for 2 minutes, then gradually add the milk and bring to the boil. Reduce the heat to simmer gently, add the sugar, cocoa and coffee, and cook until dissolved.

Turn out the pudding and pour over the hot sauce to serve.

196 BAKED GINGER PUDDING WITH LEMON SAUCE

Preparation time:
20 minutes

Cooking time:
45-50 minutes

Oven temperature:
180 C, 350 F, gas 4

Serves 4

Calories:
545 per portion

YOU WILL NEED:
100 g/4 oz soft margarine
100 g/4 oz soft brown sugar
2 eggs, lightly beaten
175 g/6 oz self-raising flour, sifted
2 teaspoons ground ginger
FOR THE SAUCE
grated rind and juice of 2 lemons
25 g/1 oz cornflour
50 g/2 oz sugar
300 ml/½ pint water
25 g/1 oz butter

Grease a deep 15 cm/6 inch square cake tin. Beat the margarine and sugar together until creamy, gradually beat in the eggs, then fold in the flour and ginger. Pour into the tin and bake in a moderate oven for 40-45 mintues. Turn out of the tin.

To make the sauce, mix the lemon rind and juice with the cornflour and sugar. Gradually add the water, transfer to the hob and bring to the boil, stirring continuously. Stir in the butter. Cut the pudding into squares and serve it hot with the sauce.

■ MICROWAVE TIP

Steamed puddings microwave well. Cover with microwave cling film instead of foil. Microwave on full power for 5 minutes.

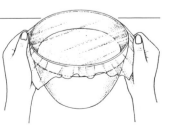

■ MICROWAVE TIP

To make lemon sauce in the microwave, mix ingredients until smooth, adding all the liquid. Microwave on full power 6 minutes, whisking twice.

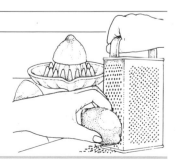

197 SPICED BREAD AND BUTTER PUDDING

Preparation time:
10 minutes, plus 10 minutes to soak

Cooking time:
1 hour

Oven temperature:
180 C, 350 F, gas 4

Serves 4

Calories:
435 per portion

YOU WILL NEED:
50 g/2 oz butter
8 slices white bread, crusts removed
100 g/4 oz mixed dried fruit
50 g/2 oz demerara sugar
600 ml/1 pint milk
2 eggs, lightly beaten
1 teaspoon mixed spice
grated nutmeg and demerara sugar, to sprinkle on the top

Butter each slice of bread generously and cut into four squares. Place a layer of bread over the base of a 1.5 litre/2½ pint ovenproof dish, overlapping the slices. Sprinkle with mixed dried fruit and continue to make alternate layers of bread and fruit.

Dissolve the sugar in the milk over a low heat. Remove from the heat, gradually add the egg and mixed spice. Whisk thoroughly. Pour the mixture over the bread and fruit mixture and leave to soak for about 10 minutes. Sprinkle the top with nutmeg and bake in a moderate oven for 1 hour. Sprinkle with sugar and serve immediately.

198 MARMALADE SPONGE PUDDING

Preparation time:
15 minutes

Cooking time:
1½-2 hours

Serves 4

Calories:
505 per portion

YOU WILL NEED:
100 g/4 oz butter or margarine, softened
100 g/4 oz soft brown sugar
grated rind of 1 orange
2 eggs, lightly beaten
175 g/6 oz self-raising flour, sifted
2 tablespoons orange marmalade

Grease a 1 litre/2 pint pudding basin. Beat the butter or margarine with the sugar until pale and creamy. Beat in the orange rind. Gradually beat in the eggs. Using a metal spoon, fold in the flour.

Spoon the marmalade into the bottom of the pudding basin and spoon the sponge mixture on top. Cover with a double thickness of greased greaseproof paper, folding a pleat to allow the pudding to rise. Tie tightly. Steam on a trivet or upturned saucer in a saucepan half-full of water for 1½-2 hours. Turn out and serve immediately with hot custard.

■ COOK'S TIP

Bread and butter pudding is a good dish in which to use up stale bread. Wholemeal bread can also be used.

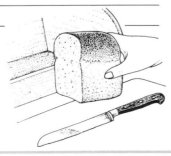

■ COOK'S TIP

For a traditional jam sponge pudding, replace the soft brown sugar with caster sugar, omit the orange rind and replace the marmalade with jam.

To make a plain fruit pudding, use caster sugar instead of brown sugar, then fold in 50 g/2 oz dried mixed fruit with the flour. Omit the marmalade.

199 PINEAPPLE UPSIDE-DOWN PUDDING

Preparation time: 15 minutes	YOU WILL NEED: 25 g/1 oz butter
	50 g/2 oz soft brown sugar
Cooking time: 50 minutes	1 × 227g/8 oz can pineapple rings, drained
Oven temperature: 180 C, 0 F, gas 4	4 glacé cherries, halved FOR THE SPONGE
	100 g/4 oz butter, softened
Serves 4	100 g/4 oz caster sugar
	2 eggs, lightly beaten
Calories: 610 per portion	¼ teaspoon mixed spice
	175 g/6 oz self-raising flour, sifted

Lightly grease a 15 cm/6 inch round cake tin. Melt the butter in a saucepan, add the sugar and pour over the base of the tin. Arrange the pineapple rings and cherries decoratively in the base, placing the cherries rounded side down.

To make the sponge mixture, beat the butter and sugar until soft and creamy. Gradually beat in the eggs and using a metal spoon, fold in the spice and flour. Spoon the mixture over the fruit in the tin, carefully smooth the top and bake in a moderate oven for about 50 minutes or until the sponge is firm and golden.

Turn out the sponge on to a serving plate, and serve immediately with custard or cream.

200 PRUNE AND APRICOT PUDDING

Preparation time: 10 minutes	YOU WILL NEED: 100 g/4 oz no-need-to-soak stoned dried prunes
Cooking time: 1 hour	100 g/4 oz no-need-to-soak dried apricots
Oven temperature: 180 C, 350 F, gas 4	4 tablespoons water 50 g/2 oz chopped walnuts FOR THE SPONGE
Serves 4	100 g/4 oz soft margarine
	100 g/4 oz soft brown sugar
Calories: 550 per portion	2 eggs, lightly beaten
	100 g/4 oz self-raising wholemeal flour

Arrange the prunes and apricots in the base of a 1.2 litre/2 pint ovenproof dish. Sprinkle over the water and add the walnuts. Beat the margarine and sugar together until creamy. Gradually beat in the eggs, then fold in the flour. The mixture should be a soft dropping consistency. Cover the fruit with the sponge mixture and bake for about an hour in a moderate oven. Serve hot with custard.

■ COOK'S TIP

Other canned fruits can be used in this recipe. Try apricot halves, peach halves or slices, or pear halves.

If you like, make a quick jam sauce to serve with the pudding. Heat 225 g/8 oz jam in a saucepan with the juice from the fruit. Stir to prevent sticking, then strain before serving.

■ MICROWAVE TIP

Cover dried fruit with water or fruit juice, cover with microwave cling film and microwave on full power for about 18 minutes instead of soaking.

201 APPLE AND APRICOT CHARLOTTE

Preparation time:
20 minutes

Cooking time:
50-60 minutes

Oven temperature:
180 C, 350 F, gas 4

Serves 4

Calories:
300 per portion

YOU WILL NEED:
7 × 1 cm/½ inch slices white bread
50 g/2 oz butter
2 large cooking apples
1 × 425 g/15 oz can apricot pie filling
50 g/2 oz soft brown or demerara
  sugar
½ teaspoon ground cinnamon
knob of butter

Remove the crusts from the bread and use two slices to make breadcrumbs. Butter the remaining slices and use to line a 1.2 litre/2 pint ovenproof dish (buttered sides against the dish), cutting them to fit.

Peel, core and chop the apples. Mix with the apricot pie filling and spoon into the lined dish. Mix together the bread-crumbs, sugar and cinnamon and sprinkle over the top. Dot a knob of butter over the top and bake in a moderate oven for 50-60 minutes. Serve hot with custard or fresh cream.

202 RHUBARB CRUMBLE

Preparation time:
15 minutes

Cooking time:
40 minutes

Oven temperature:
180 C, 350 F, gas 4

Serves 4

Calories:
445 per portion

YOU WILL NEED:
450 g/1 lb rhubarb
75 g/3 oz soft brown sugar
grated rind of 1 orange
FOR THE CRUMBLE
75 g/3 oz butter
175 g/6 oz plain flour
75 g/3 oz soft brown sugar

Wash and trim the rhubarb. Cut the stalks into 2.5 cm/1 inch lengths and put into a buttered 900 ml/1½ pint pie dish. Sprinkle over the sugar and orange rind.

To make the crumble, rub the butter into the flour until the mixture resembles fine breadcrumbs. Stir in the sugar and spread the crumble over the rhubarb mixture, smoothing it over to cover the fruit completely. Bake in a moderate oven for about 40 minutes or until the crumble is crunchy and golden and the fruit is cooked. Serve the crumble hot with vanilla ice cream.

■ COOK'S TIP

Instead of using the apricot pie filling, double the quantity of apples and add 50 g/2 oz raisins to make a simple apple charlotte.

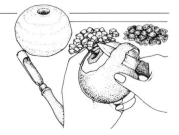

■ COOK'S TIP

Ginger complements rhubarb. Chop about 4 pieces crystallized or preserved stem ginger and add to the rhubarb.

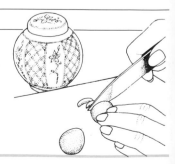

203 RICE PUDDING

Preparation time:
5 minutes

Cooking time:
1½ hours

Oven temperature:
160C, 325F, gas 3

Serves 4

Calories:
180 per portion

YOU WILL NEED:
600 ml/1 pint milk
40 g/1½ oz short-grain rice
few drops vanilla essence
40 g/1½ oz caster sugar
knob of butter

Bring the milk to the boil in a saucepan, then lower the heat, add the rice, vanilla essence and sugar. Simmer gently for a few minutes. Transfer to an ovenproof dish, top with the butter and cook in a moderate oven for 1½ hours. Serve either hot or cold.

There are many variations of rice pudding. For instance you can make a more creamy pudding by adding 150 ml/¼ pint cream, a spicy one by adding ¼ teaspoon each nutmeg and cinnamon, or you can serve the pudding with a spoonful of warmed jam on each portion.

204 SEMOLINA SWIRL PUDDING

Preparation time:
5 minutes

Cooking time:
15 minutes

Serves 4

Calories:
265 per portion

YOU WILL NEED:
600 ml/1 pint milk
50 g/2 oz caster or granulated sugar
50 g/2 oz semolina
4 generous teaspoons chocolate hazelnut spread
1 tablespoon chopped mixed nuts

Heat the milk and sugar gently, sprinkle in the semolina and bring slowly to the boil. Simmer gently for 10-15 minutes, stirring constantly until the mixture is thickened and cooked.

Turn out into individual bowls, carefully swirl one teaspoon of chocolate hazelnut spread into each pudding. Sprinkle over the chopped nuts and serve immediately.

■ COOK'S TIP

When time is short, simply stir all the ingredients together in an ovenproof dish and bake, allowing an extra 15 minutes.

■ COOK'S TIP

For a speedy dessert, turn canned semolina pudding into a serving dish. Chill in the freezer, then swirl the chocolate hazelnut spread through and serve.

205 MINCE PIES

Preparation time:
20 minutes

Cooking time:
15-20 minutes

Oven temperature:
200 C, 400 F, gas 6

Makes 12

Calories:
140 per pie

YOU WILL NEED:
225 g/8 oz plain flour
pinch of salt
100 g/4 oz margarine
2-3 tablespoons cold water
icing sugar, to dust
FOR THE FILLING
225 g/8 oz mincemeat
1-2 tablespoons brandy

Sift the flour and salt into a bowl. Cut the margarine into small pieces and rub into the flour until the mixture resembles fine breadcrumbs. Mix to a firm dough with water.

Roll out the pastry thinly on a lightly floured work surface and, using fluted cutters, stamp out 12 7 cm/2¾ inch rounds and 12 5.5 cm/2¼ inch rounds.

Place the larger rounds in lightly greased tartlet tins. Mix the mincemeat with the brandy and place a teaspoonful in each pastry case. Dampen the edges of the pastry with a little water and cover with a pastry lid. Seal the edges and snip two slots in the top of each pie. Bake in a moderately hot oven for 15-20 minutes or until golden brown. Dust with icing sugar and serve hot or cold with cream.

206 BLACKBERRY AND APPLE PIE

Preparation time:
20 minutes

Cooking time:
45-50 minutes

Oven temperature:
180 C, 350 F, gas 4

Serves 4

Calories:
485 per portion

YOU WILL NEED:
175 g/6 oz plain flour
pinch of salt
100 g/4 oz margarine
25 g/1 oz caster sugar
1 teaspoon grated lemon rind
1 egg yolk
milk, to glaze
FOR THE FILLING
225 g/8 oz cooking apples, peeled,
cored and sliced
225 g/8 oz fresh or frozen blackberries,
hulled or defrosted
75 g/3 oz caster sugar

Sift the flour and salt into a bowl. Cut the margarine into small pieces and rub in until the mixture resembles fine breadcrumbs. Mix in the sugar, lemon rind and egg yolk to form a dough. Knead lightly.

Spoon the apples and blackberries into a 900 ml/1½ pints pie dish and sprinkle over the sugar. Roll out the pastry to cover the pie. Cut a strip from the outside and place on the dampened rim of the pie dish. Brush the pastry strip with water and lift on the lid to cover the pie. Seal and flute the edges with the blunt edge of a knife. Decorate with any pastry trimmings, glaze with milk and bake in a moderate oven for 45-50 minutes.

■ COOK'S TIP

To make the pies extra special, add the grated rind of 1 orange to the pastry, with the flour.

■ COOK'S TIP

Use cocktail cutters to cut out pastry shapes to decorate the top of the pie.

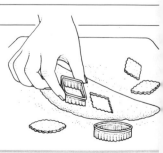

207 TREACLE TART

Preparation time:	YOU WILL NEED:
15 minutes	225 g/8 oz plain flour
	pinch of salt
Cooking time:	100 g/4 oz margarine
35 minutes	2-3 tablespoons cold water
Oven temperature:	FOR THE FILLING
190 C, 375 F, gas 5	8 tablespoons golden syrup
	2 teaspoons grated lemon rind
Serves 4	50 g/2 oz fresh white breadcrumbs
Calories:	
575 per portion	

Sift the flour and salt into a bowl. Cut the margarine into small pieces and rub in until the mixture resembles fine breadcrumbs. Sprinkle over the water and mix to form a dough. Knead very lightly, roll out three-quarters of the pastry on a lightly floured surface and use to line a 23 cm/9 inch ovenproof pie plate. Leave to chill in the refrigerator while preparing the filling.

Gently heat the syrup and mix in the lemon rind and breadcrumbs. Pour into the pastry shell. Roll out the remaining pastry and cut into thin strips to form a lattice pattern on top of the tart. Bake in a moderately hot oven for about 30 minutes and serve with a custard sauce.

208 CUSTARD JAM TART

Preparation time:	YOU WILL NEED:
20 minutes	225 g/8 oz plain flour
	pinch of salt
Cooking time:	100 g/4 oz margarine
1 hour 10 minutes	2-3 tablespoons cold water
Oven temperature:	FOR THE FILLING
200 C, 400 F, gas 6	2 tablespoons jam
and	600 ml/1 pint milk
160 C, 325 F, gas 3	50 g/2 oz caster sugar, plus extra to
	sprinkle
Serves 4	4 egg yolks
Calories:	few drops vanilla essence
625 per portion	½ teaspoon grated nutmeg

Sift the flour and salt into a bowl. Cut the margarine into small pieces and rub in until the mixture resembles fine breadcrumbs. Add the water and mix to form a dough. Knead very lightly, roll out on a lightly floured surface and use to line a 20 cm/8 inch fluted flan ring placed on a baking tray. Prick the base with a fork and bake blind in a moderately hot oven for 10 minutes.

Spread the jam evenly over the pastry. Heat the milk over a low heat until lukewarm, then beat in the sugar, egg yolks and vanilla. Pour over the jam, sprinkle the nutmeg on top and bake in a moderate oven for about 1 hour until firm. Serve either hot or cold, sprinkled with a little extra caster sugar.

■ MICROWAVE TIP

Put the syrup in a basin and microwave on full power for 1½-2 minutes, then mix in the lemon rind and breadcrumbs.

■ FREEZER TIP

Open freeze an extra pastry flan case, then pack the middle with crumpled absorbent kitchen paper, put in a polythene bag and freeze. Cook from frozen.

209 APPLE STRUDEL

Preparation time:
20 minutes

Cooking time:
25-30 minutes

Oven temperature:
200 C, 400 F, gas 6

Serves 4

Calories:
540 per portion

YOU WILL NEED:
1 × 212 g/7½ oz packet frozen puff
 pastry, defrosted
icing sugar, to sprinkle
FOR THE FILLING
50 g/2 oz fresh white breadcrumbs
50 g/2 oz chopped walnuts
100 g/4 oz mixed dried fruit
50 g/2 oz caster sugar
450 g/1 lb cooking apples, peeled,
 cored and sliced
1 teaspoon mixed spice
grated rind of 1 orange
50 g/2 oz butter, melted

Roll out the pastry very thinly on a lightly floured board to make an oblong shape.

Mix the breadcrumbs, walnuts, dried fruit, sugar, apples, mixed spice and orange rind together, and spread over one end of the pastry to within 1 cm/½ inch of the edges. Brush the edges with the melted butter and roll up like a Swiss roll. Place on a baking tray and brush with the remainder of the butter. Bake in a moderately hot oven for 25-30 minutes or until golden.

Dust with icing sugar, slice and serve hot with custard.

210 BAKED STUFFED APPLES

Preparation time:
10 minutes

Cooking time:
40-50 minutes

Oven temperature:
180 C, 350 F, gas 4

Serves 4

Calories:
160 per portion

YOU WILL NEED:
4 large cooking apples
50 g/2 oz currants or sultanas
25 g/1 oz soft brown sugar
4 teaspoons golden syrup
½ teaspoon ground ginger
25 g/1 oz butter

Remove the cores from the apples using a corer. Slit the skin round the centre of each apple with the tip of a sharp knife to prevent the apples bursting during cooking. Place in an ovenproof dish. Mix together the fruit and sugar, and stuff the apple centres with the mixture. Pour one teaspoon of syrup over each apple, sprinkle over a little ginger and top with a knob of butter.

Bake in a moderate oven for 40-50 minutes. Serve immediately with hot custard.

■ COOK'S TIP

Use phyllo instead of puff pastry. It is sold frozen in paper-thin sheets. Brush each sheet with melted butter and use two or three sheets' thickness.

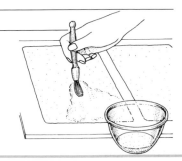

■ COOK'S TIP

If the apple core does not run straight through the middle, push the corer through from one end first, then from the other to remove all the bits.

211 TROPICAL PANCAKES

Preparation time:
20 minutes

Cooking time:
30 minutes

Oven temperature:
180°C, 350°F, gas 4

Serves 4

Calories:
475 per portion

YOU WILL NEED:
100 g/4 oz plain flour
pinch of salt
1 egg, lightly beaten
300 ml/½ pint milk
oil for frying
FOR THE FILLING
50 g/2 oz butter
25 g/1 oz dark soft brown sugar, plus
    extra for sprinkling
6 ripe bananas, roughly chopped
2 tablespoons dark rum
juice of 1 lemon
25 g/1 oz flaked almonds

Sift the flour and salt into a bowl. Add the egg, then gradually half the milk, beating well to make a smooth batter. Beat in the remaining milk.

Heat a little oil in a frying pan. Pour in a little batter, tilting the pan so the batter covers the base, and cook until the underside is golden. Turn and cook the second side, then remove and keep warm. Repeat with the remaining batter.

Melt the butter in a frying pan with the sugar. Stir in the bananas and cook until softened, add the rum and lemon juice and mix thoroughly. Place one pancake on a greased ovenproof plate. Cover with a little banana mixture and then another pancake. Continue layering in this way, and sprinkle the last pancake with sugar and flaked almonds. Bake in a moderate oven for 12-15 minutes. Serve hot, cut into wedges.

212 PINEAPPLE AND APRICOT FRITTERS

Preparation time:
15 minutes

Cooking time:
5 minutes

Serves 4

Calories:
415 per portion

YOU WILL NEED:
1 × 425 g/15 oz can pineapple rings
1 × 410 g/14 oz can apricot halves
flour for dusting
oil for deep frying
FOR THE BATTER
100 g/4 oz plain flour
pinch of mixed spice
pinch of salt
1 large egg, separated
150 ml/¼ pint water
1 tablespoon oil
caster sugar, to sprinkle

Drain the pineapple rings and apricot halves, pat dry with absorbent kitchen paper and dust with flour. Sift the flour, mixed spice and salt into a bowl. Gradually beat in the egg yolk, water and oil to form a smooth batter. Whisk the egg white until stiff and fold in.

Heat the oil for deep frying to 180 C/350 F, or until a cube of bread dropped in becomes golden in 30 seconds. Dip the pieces of fruit into the batter to coat well and fry the fritters for 4-5 minutes or until golden. Drain on absorbent kitchen paper. Sprinkle with sugar and serve immediately with cream.

■ COOK'S TIP

To create a pyramid effect, make each pancake slightly smaller than the last, by using a little less batter. When assembling, start with the largest pancake.

■ COOK'S TIP

Use peeled bananas, cut in half, instead of the canned fruit. Serve with a little warmed golden syrup poured over.

213 CHOCOLATE FONDUE WITH FRESH FRUIT

Preparation time:
15 minutes

Cooking time:
3-5 minutes

Serves 4

Calories:
570 per portion

YOU WILL NEED:
2 kiwi fruit
225 g/8 oz fresh strawberries
225 g/8 oz grapes
100 g/4 oz fresh or canned pineapple
  segments
100 g/4 oz fresh or canned satsuma
  segments
FOR THE FONDUE
225 g/8 oz plain chocolate
150 ml/¼ pint double cream
2 tablespoons brandy

Peel the kiwi fruit and cut each into four. Hull the strawberries. Arrange all the fruit attractively in serving bowls.

Melt the chocolate gently either in a fondue pan or in a basin over simmering water, when completely melted gradually add the cream and brandy, stirring well. Transfer the fondue to the table and keep hot over a burner.

Dip the fruit in the fondue, using fondue forks.

214 BLACK CHERRY CLAFOUTI

Preparation time:
15 minutes

Cooking time:
50-60 minutes

Oven temperature:
190°C, 375°F, gas 5

Serves 4

Calories:
545 per portion

YOU WILL NEED:
2 × 411 g/14½ oz cans stoned black
  cherries, well drained
175 g/6 oz plain flour
100 g/4 oz caster sugar, plus extra to
  sprinkle
4 eggs
600 ml/1 pint milk

Lightly grease a 1.5 litre/2½ pint shallow ovenproof dish. Spread the drained cherries over the bottom.

Place the flour and sugar in a bowl, make a well in the centre and add the eggs and milk. Gradually work the flour into the liquid to make a smooth batter. Pour over the cherries and bake in a moderately hot oven for 50-60 minutes, or until golden brown and firm to the touch. Sprinkle with caster sugar and serve warm with cream.

■ MICROWAVE TIP

Melt the chocolate in a basin in the microwave on full power for about 3-4 minutes. Stir in the cream and brandy, microwave for 30 seconds and serve.

■ COOK'S TIP

To make batter in the food processor, put in the flour, eggs and a little milk. Process until smooth, then gradually add the remaining milk as the machine works.

215 PEARS IN GINGER WINE

Preparation time:
5-10 minutes

Cooking time:
25-35 minutes

Serves 4

Calories:
120 per portion

YOU WILL NEED:
450 g/1 lb cooking pears
juice and rind of 1 lemon
300 ml/½ pint ginger wine
½ teaspoon ground cinnamon
50 g/2 oz sugar
angelica, to decorate

Peel the pears but leave their stalks in place. Brush the fruit with some of the lemon juice to prevent discolouring. Slowly bring the wine to the boil in a large saucepan, reduce the heat, add the pears, cinnamon and sugar and simmer gently for 20-30 minutes or until the pears are soft. Baste the pears from time to time and turn once during cooking. When the pears are soft, remove them to a serving dish and decorate the top of each with pieces of angelica.

Boil the wine remaining in the saucepan, if necessary, until it is reduced to a syrup consistency. Spoon the syrup over the pears and serve immediately with fresh cream.

216 HOT FRUIT SALAD

Preparation time:
20 minutes

Cooking time:
10-12 minutes

Serves 4

Calories:
230 per portion

YOU WILL NEED:
2 bananas
2 dessert apples
2 oranges
225 g/8 oz black grapes
100 g/4 oz seedless grapes
150 ml/¼ pint apple juice
25 g/1 oz butter
½ teaspoon ginger
½ teaspoon grated nutmeg
½ teaspoon ground cinnamon
2 tablespoons honey
1 lemon, quartered

Peel and slice the bananas. Core and slice the apples. Peel the oranges, remove the pith and cut oranges into segments. Halve the black grapes and remove the pips. Put all the fruit in a bowl with the apple juice.

Melt the butter in a large saucepan over a gentle heat. Add the spices and honey and mix thoroughly, warming through. Add the fruit salad mixture and the lemon and cook for 8-10 minutes, stirring occasionally. Remove the lemon and serve the fruit salad immediately with clotted or double cream.

■ MICROWAVE TIP

Pears in wine microwave very well. Place ingredients in a dish, stir, cover and cook on full power for about 10 minutes.

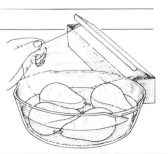

■ COOK'S TIP

Trim the ends off the orange, stand the fruit on a board, then cut downwards to remove strips of peel and pith all at once.

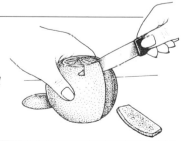

COOL DESSERTS

Choose a dessert to complement the meal, something light and lemony after a rich pork or duck dish, a crisp pie or tart after fish, or a chocolate dessert after chicken. This chapter includes favourite traditional recipes like trifle, as well as more unusual chocolate mint cheesecake and yogurt fool.

217 CHILLED STRAWBERRY CREAMS

Preparation time:
10 minutes, plus 1
hour to chill

Serves 6

Calories:
500 per portion

YOU WILL NEED:
225 g/8 oz strawberries
600 ml/1 pint double cream
50 g/2 oz caster sugar
1 tablespoon brandy

Slice the strawberries. Whip the cream until thick, fold in the strawberries, sugar and brandy.

Spoon into individual glasses and chill for at least 1 hour.

218 POTS AU CHOCOLAT

Preparation time:
15 minutes, plus 1½
hours to chill

Serves 4

Calories:
615 per portion

YOU WILL NEED:
50 g/2 oz butter
225 g/8 oz plain chocolate
2 eggs
2 tablespoons rum
150 ml/¼ pint double cream
FOR THE DECORATION
whipped cream
grated chocolate or chocolate caraque

Melt the butter and chocolate in a bowl over a saucepan of simmering water. Remove the bowl from the heat, beat in the eggs and rum, leave to cool. Whip the cream until stiff and fold into the chocolate mixture. Pour the mixture into four ramekin dishes, chill until set.

Decorate with rosettes of piped cream and chocolate caraque (see Cook's Tip below) just before serving.

■ COOK'S TIP

Make creamy banana splits by serving the strawberry cream in split bananas. Top with chopped toasted hazelnuts and grated chocolate.

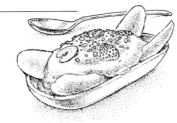

■ COOK'S TIP

To make chocolate caraque (or long curls), take a block of chocolate and a fairly sharp knife. Holding the knife at an acute angle, shave long curls off the chocolate. Turn *the block round when you have made a deep groove and work from the opposite end. See also, Cook's Tip, recipe 236.*

219 QUICK LEMON MOUSSE

Preparation time:
10 minutes, plus 1
hour to chill

Cooking time:
2-3 minutes

Serves 4

Calories:
250 per portion

YOU WILL NEED:
2 lemons
1 lemon jelly
150 ml/¼ pint water
1 × 410 g/14½ oz can evaporated milk
angelica, to decorate

Reserve four slices of lemon for decoration. Grate the rind from one lemon and extract the juice from both. Melt the jelly in the water over a gentle heat. Remove the pan from the heat, add the lemon rind and juice. Pour into a small bowl and leave to cool.

Whisk the evaporated milk until thick and doubled in volume. Carefully fold in the jelly mixture and pour into a large glass dish. Chill for about an hour or until set. Decorate with the lemon slices and pieces of angelica.

220 CITRUS SYLLABUB

Preparation time:
15 minutes, plus 1
hour to marinate
and 1 hour to chill

Serves 6

Calories:
290 per portion

YOU WILL NEED:
grated rind and juice of 1 orange
grated rind and juice of 1 lemon
4 tablespoons sweet white wine
75 g/3 oz caster sugar
300 ml/½ pint double cream, whipped

Place the fruit rinds and juices in a bowl with the wine and marinate for at least 1 hour. Strain the liquid through a fine sieve, reserving a few strands of rind for decoration.

Gently fold the strained liquid and sugar into the cream. Spoon into six glass serving dishes. Decorate with the citrus rind and chill for an hour before serving. Serve with brandy snaps or sweet biscuits of your choice.

FREEZER TIP

Double or whipping cream can be frozen in its whipped state. Spoon it into a plastic container and label with the quantity of unwhipped cream.

COOK'S TIP

Syllabub makes a luscious topping for a traditional trifle. Swirl it over the top of the custard, or it can even be used instead of the custard.

221 RHUBARB FOOL

Preparation time:
10 minutes, plus 1
hour to chill

Cooking time:
10-15 minutes

Serves 4

Calories:
345 per portion

YOU WILL NEED:
450 g/1 lb rhubarb
50 g/2 oz soft brown sugar
1 × 425 g/15 oz can custard
150 ml/¼ pint double cream
chocolate shavings, to decorate

Wash the rhubarb and cut into 2.5 cm/1 inch lengths. Place in a saucepan with the sugar, cover and cook gently for 10-15 minutes until the rhubarb is softened. Blend the rhubarb and custard together in a liquidizer or food processor until smooth.

Whip the cream until stiff, fold into the cooled rhubarb mixture and pour into individual glass dishes. Chill for about an hour and decorate with chocoate shavings and biscuits, such as cigarettes russes, shown above.

222 YOGURT FOOL

Preparation time:
10 minutes, plus 2
hours to chill

Serves 4

Calories:
285 per portion

YOU WILL NEED:
300 ml/½ pint whipping cream
150 ml/¼ pint natural yogurt
50 g/2 oz soft brown sugar
50 g/2 oz muesli
50 g/2 oz chopped walnuts

Whip the cream until it stands in soft peaks. Fold in the yogurt and carefully spoon into individual glass dishes. Sprinkle generously with the sugar, muesli and walnuts.

Chill for about 2 hours.

■ MICROWAVE TIP

*Cook the rhubarb and sugar
in a covered dish in the
microwave. Allow about
8-10 minutes on full power.*

■ COOK'S TIP

*If you are trying to cut
down on the fat content of
your diet, then simply stir
all the ingredients into
natural yogurt.*

223 FROZEN RASPBERRY DELIGHT

Preparation time:
10 minutes, plus 2 hours to freeze

Serves 4

Calories:
595 per portion

YOU WILL NEED:
1 Swiss roll
3 tablespoons brandy
300 ml/½ pint raspberry yogurt
100 g/4 oz fresh or frozen raspberries, hulled or defrosted
300 ml/½ pint double or whipping cream
whipped cream, to decorate

Slice the Swiss roll thinly and use to line the base and sides of a 900 ml/1½ pint pudding basin. Carefully spoon over the brandy.

In a bowl, mix together the yogurt and raspberries. Whip the cream until thick and fold into the yogurt mixture. Pour over the Swiss roll and freeze for 2 hours or until firm.

Dip the basin briefly in warm water to help turn out the pudding. Decorate with piped whipped cream and serve immediately.

224 CHOCOLATE ORANGE SOUFFLE

Preparation time:
30 minutes, plus 1 hour to chill

Cooking time:
5 minutes

Serves 6

Calories:
480 per portion

YOU WILL NEED:
3 eggs, separated
75 g/3 oz caster sugar
grated rind and juice of 2 oranges
15 g/½ oz gelatine
3 tablespoons hot water
300 ml/½ pint whipping cream
175 g/6 oz plain chocolate, grated

Lightly grease a 600 ml/1 pint soufflé dish. Cut a double strip of greaseproof paper, equal in width to the height of the dish plus 5cm/2 inches and long enough to go right round the outside of the dish. Lightly grease the top 5 cm/2 inches and tie securely with string around the dish.

Place the egg yolks and sugar in a bowl over a saucepan of simmering water and whisk until thick and creamy. Whisk in the orange rind and juice. Dissolve the gelatine in the water over simmering water.

Whisk the egg whites until they stand in soft peaks and whip the cream until stiff. Fold the cooled gelatine into the orange mixture, followed by half the cream, the egg whites and two-thirds of the grated chocolate. Pour into the soufflé dish, smooth the top and chill until set.

Peel the paper away from the soufflé and press grated chocolate around the sides. With the remaining cream pipe swirls on the top and decorate with grated chocolate.

■ FREEZER TIP

Pipe swirls of whipped cream on to a cling film lined baking tray. Open freeze, pack in rigid containers and use from frozen to decorate cakes.

■ MICROWAVE TIP

Gelatine can be dissolved in the water, in a small basin in the microwave. Allow about 1 minute on full power.

225 BAKED ALASKA

Preparation time:
15 minutes

Cooking time:
3-5 minutes

Oven temperature:
230 C, 450 F, gas 8

Serves 4

Calories:
695 per portion

YOU WILL NEED:
*1 bought or home-made 20 cm/8 inch
    sponge flan case*
1 tablespoon sherry
*1 × 1 litre/35.2 fl oz block raspberry
    ripple ice cream*
3 egg whites
150 g/5 oz caster sugar

Place the sponge flan case on a baking tray and sprinkle over the sherry. Scoop the ice cream on to the sponge and smooth over with a knife to make an even round. Freeze to harden again.

Whisk the egg whites until they form stiff peaks. Whisk in the sugar a little at a time. The mixture should be thick and glossy. Quickly spoon or pipe the meringue on to the ice cream and sponge to cover it completely. Bake in a hot oven for 3-5 minutes until the meringue is golden. Serve immediately.

226 LEMON MERINGUE PIE

Preparation time:
30 minutes

Cooking time:
35 minutes

Oven temperature:
200 C, 400 F, gas 6
and
180 C, 350 F, gas 4

Serves 6

Calories:
375 per portion

YOU WILL NEED:
*¾ × recipe shortcrust pastry (recipe
    176)*
FOR THE LEMON FILLING
grated rind and juice of 2 lemons
25 g/1 oz cornflour
300 ml/½ pint water
25 g/1 oz butter
75 g/3 oz caster sugar
2 egg yolks
FOR THE MERINGUE TOPPING
2 egg whites
100 g/4 oz caster sugar
*glacé cherries and angelica, to
    decorate*

Make the shortcrust pastry as instructed in recipe 176, roll out to line a 20 cm/8 inch flan ring placed on a baking tray. Prick with a fork and bake blind (see Cook's Tip 179) in a moderately hot oven for 15 minutes.

Put the lemon rind and juice in a saucepan with the cornflour, add the water and bring slowly to the boil and cook for 2 minutes, stirring all the time. Remove from the heat and add the butter and sugar. Cool slightly, then stir in the egg yolks and spoon into the flan case.

Whisk the egg whites until stiff but not dry, gradually whisk in the sugar. Pipe or spoon the meringue over the lemon filling. Bake in a moderate oven for 15 minutes and serve decorated with pieces of cherry and angelica.

■ FREEZER TIP

The baked alaska can be prepared in advance, covered with meringue, then open frozen ready to be put in the oven at the last minute.

■ COOK'S TIP

Any citrus fruits or combination of fruits can be used. Substitute 3 limes for the lemons. An orange and lemon mix is delicious, substitute an orange for one *of the lemons. When using larger fruits, such as grapefruit use 1 tablespoon of grated rind and reduce the water.*

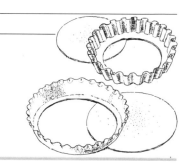

227 MANDARIN TARTLETS

Preparation time:
20 minutes

Cooking time:
20 minutes

Oven temperature:
190 C, 375 F, gas 5

Makes 12

Calories:
195 per tartlet

YOU WILL NEED:
200 g/7 oz plain flour
pinch of salt
75 g/3 oz butter or margarine
25 g/1 oz caster sugar
1 egg
FOR THE TOPPING
150 ml/¼ pint double or whipping
  cream
2 × 312 g/11 oz cans mandarins,
  drained
2 tablespoons orange marmalade
1 tablespoon water

Sift the flour and salt into a bowl. Rub in the fat until the mixture resembles fine breadcrumbs. Stir in the sugar and egg and knead lightly to form a smooth soft dough. Roll out on a floured work surface to 3 mm/⅛ inch thickness and, using a 6 cm/2½ inch fluted cutter, stamp out 12 circles. Use to line a tray of 12 tartlet tins, prick the bases with a fork and bake in a moderate oven for 20 minutes or until lightly browned. Leave to cool.

Whip the cream until stiff, place a spoonful in each tartlet and smooth the surface. Arrange the mandarins on each tartlet. Heat the marmalade with the water over a gentle heat until melted. Cool slightly and brush over the mandarins. Place on a pretty plate to serve.

228 STRAWBERRY SHORTBREAD CREAMS

Preparation time:
20 minutes

Cooking time:
45-50 minutes

Oven temperature:
160 C, 325 F, gas 3

Serves 4

Calories:
570 per portion

YOU WILL NEED:
100 g/4 oz butter
175 g/6 oz plain flour
50 g/2 oz caster sugar
grated rind of 1 orange
FOR THE FILLING
150 ml/¼ pint double or whipping
  cream
225 g/8 oz strawberries, halved

Grease a 20 cm/8 inch fluted flan ring and a baking tray. Rub the butter into the flour. Add the sugar and orange rind, knead the mixture together until it forms a soft dough.

Turn out on to a lightly floured surface and roll to a circle large enough to fill the flan ring. Place in the flan ring on the baking tray, press into the fluted edges and smooth the top. Prick all over with a fork and mark into eight equal portions. Bake in a moderate oven for 45-50 minutes. Leave the shortbread to cool in the flan ring for 10 minutes, then cut into eight.

Whip the cream until stiff. Spoon or pipe the cream on to four pieces of shortbread, add the strawberries to the cream and top with a second piece of shortbread.

■ COOK'S TIP

There is no need to grease baking tins when cooking pastry because of the high fat content of the dough. In some recipes if the filling is likely to stick the tins may be greased.

Dampen baking trays for puff and choux pastry items which are unlikely to stick. The moisture gives a better rise.

■ COOK'S TIP

If you do not have a flan ring, then use a loose-bottomed flan tin or cake tin to cook the shortbread.

231 FRESH FRUIT PAVLOVA

Preparation time:
30 minutes

Cooking time:
1 hour

Oven temperature:
150°C, 300°F, gas 2

Serves 6

Calories:
410 per portion

YOU WILL NEED:
3 egg whites
175 g/6 oz caster sugar
1 teaspoon cornflour
1 teaspoon vinegar
½ teaspoon vanilla essence
FOR THE FILLING
300 ml/½ pint double cream
2 bananas, sliced and brushed with
*   lemon juice*
2 kiwi fruits, peeled and sliced
100 g/4 oz green grapes, halved and
*   seeded*
2 oranges, peeled and segmented

Mark a 20 cm/8 inch circle on a piece of non-stick baking parchment and place on a baking tray. Whisk the egg whites until they stand in stiff peaks. Gradually whisk in half the sugar. Fold in the remaining sugar with the cornflour, vinegar and vanilla. Spoon or pipe the meringue on to the marked circle and bake in the centre of a cool oven for 1 hour. Leave to cool in oven. Remove paper and place on a plate.

Whip the cream until stiff. Spoon over the pavlova base, arrange the prepared fruit on top and chill before serving.

232 MERINGUES WITH CHOCOLATE SAUCE

Preparation time:
15 minutes

Cooking time:
2½ hours

Oven temperature:
110°C, 225°F, gas ¼

Serves 6

Calories:
265 per portion

YOU WILL NEED:
4 egg whites
225 g/8 oz caster sugar
FOR THE CHOCOLATE SAUCE
150 ml/¼ pint water
50 g/2 oz sugar
4 tablespoons golden syrup
4 tablespoons cocoa powder

Grease three baking trays thoroughly or line with non-stick baking parchment. Whisk the egg whites until stiff and standing in peaks. Add the sugar, a tablespoon at a time, whisking continuously. Fit a piping bag with a large star nozzle and fill the bag with the meringue mixture.

Pipe 36 rosettes on to the baking trays or spoon on if preferred. Bake in a very cool oven for 2½ hours or until the meringues are crisp. Remove from the oven and cool on a wire rack.

To make the chocolate sauce, put all the ingredients into a pan and heat very gently. Bring to the boil, reduce the heat and cook for 1 minute, stirring all the time. Spoon over the meringues just before serving.

■ COOK'S TIP

To pipe meringues, use a large piping bag, fitted with a large plain nozzle.

■ MICROWAVE TIP

To make the chocolate sauce in the microwave, put all the ingredients in a measuring jug and microwave on full power 5 minutes, stirring once.

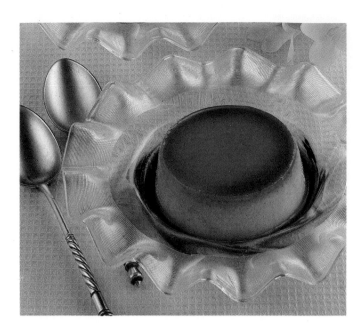

233 CREME CARAMEL

Preparation time:
15 minutes, plus 4
hours to chill

Cooking time:
1 hour 10 minutes

Oven temperature:
160 C, 325 F, gas 3

Serves 6

Calories:
175 per portion

YOU WILL NEED:
75 g/3 oz granulated sugar
3 tablespoons water
600 ml/1 pint milk
2 eggs plus 2 egg yolks
25 g/1 oz caster sugar
few drops vanilla essence

Grease six ramekin dishes. Put the granulated sugar and water in a heavy-based saucepan and heat gently until the sugar has dissolved. Bring the syrup to the boil and boil until the sugar caramelizes and turns a deep golden colour. Pour the caramel evenly into the ramekins.

Gently heat the milk to just below boiling point and remove from the heat. Lightly whisk together the eggs, caster sugar and vanilla, and gradually add the hot milk. Strain through a fine sieve and pour the custard into the ramekin dishes. Cover with oiled greaseproof paper and place in a roasting tin half-filled with hot water. Bake in a moderate oven for about 1 hour or until the custard has set. Remove from the oven and allow to cool. Chill the cooked custards for several hours or overnight, then turn out on to individual plates to serve. (Otherwise the caramel will be hard. Do not chill once turned out.)

234 TRADITIONAL TRIFLE

Preparation time:
20 minutes, plus 1
hour to chill

Cooking time:
5-10 minutes

Serves 6

Calories:
560 per portion

YOU WILL NEED:
8 trifle sponges
2 tablespoons raspberry jam
50 g/2 oz ratafia biscuits
4 tablespoons sweet sherry
225 g/8 oz fresh or frozen raspberries
    hulled or defrosted
1 tablespoon cornflour
50 g/2 oz sugar
450 ml/3/4 pint milk
3 eggs
a few drops vanilla essence
FOR THE TOPPING
300 ml/1/2 pint double cream
fresh raspberries and angelica

Split the trifle sponge cakes and spread with jam. Cut up and place in a glass serving dish. Break the ratafias into small pieces and scatter on the trifle sponges. Spoon over the sherry and leave to soak for at least 30 minutes. Top with the raspberries.

Blend cornflour and sugar to a paste with a little of the milk in a saucepan. Blend in remaining milk and bring to the boil, stirring. Cook 2 minutes. Lightly whisk eggs and vanilla essence together, pour on cornflour mixture, whisking. Pour over the trifle and leave until cold, then chill in the refrigerator for at least 1 hour.

Whip the cream until thick and spread or pipe on the trifle. Decorate with fresh raspberries and angelica.

■ COOK'S TIP

To prevent delicate dishes overheating and curdling, stand in a roasting tin, then pour in hot water from a kettle to come halfway up the inside of the tin.

■ COOK'S TIP

For a very quick custard for trifle, whip 150 ml/1/4 pint double cream and fold it into a well-chilled 425 g/15 oz can of custard. Spread over the trifle base.

235 SUMMER PUDDING

Preparation time: 20 minutes, plus overnight chilling	**YOU WILL NEED:** 225 g/8 oz blackcurrants, topped and tailed
	225 g/8 oz raspberries
Cooking time: 5 minutes	225 g/8 oz redcurrants, topped and tailed
Serves 6	175 g/6 oz sugar
	3 tablespoons water
Calories: 205 per portion	8-10 thin slices white bread, crusts removed

Put the prepared fruit in a large saucepan with the sugar and water, bring to the boil and simmer gently for 5 minutes. Leave to cool.

Line a 900 ml/1½ pint pudding basin with slices of bread, cutting the slices to fit and making sure that there are no gaps. Spoon the fruit mixture into the basin, and top with more bread slices cut to fit. Cover the pudding with a plate with a weight on it and chill in the refrigerator overnight so that the juices can penetrate through the bread.

To serve, turn out the pudding and accompany with clotted cream or hot custard.

236 BLACK FOREST GATEAU

Preparation time: 30 minutes	**YOU WILL NEED:** 3 eggs
	75 g/3 oz caster sugar
Cooking time: 40 minutes	50 g/2 oz plain flour
	25 g/1 oz cocoa powder
Oven temperature: 180 C, 350 F, gas 4	3 tablespoons kirsch
	600 ml/1 pint double or whipping cream
Makes 1 cake	1 × 390 g/13¾ oz can blackberry pie filling
Total calories: 4060	FOR THE GLACÉ ICING
	225 g/8 oz icing sugar, sifted
	25 g/1 oz cocoa powder
	2 tablespoons water
	chocolate curls, to decorate

Line and grease a deep 18 cm/7 inch round cake tin. Whisk the eggs and sugar until pale and thick. Fold in the flour and cocoa powder. Pour the mixture into the tin and bake in a moderate oven for about 40 minutes. Cool on a wire rack. Cut into three layers horizontally, and soak each layer with 1 tablespoon kirsch.

Whip the cream until thick. Sandwich the cake together with some of the cream and the pie filling. Mix the icing sugar, cocoa powder and water until smooth and pour over the top.

Pipe the remaining cream on to the side of the cake and a border on the top. Decorate with chocolate curls.

■ COOK'S TIP

When turning out any moulded dish, place a plate over the mould centrally. Invert the mould and the plate and give them both a firm jerk.

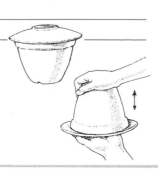

■ COOK'S TIP

To make chocolate curls, spread melted chocolate on a level smooth surface and leave to set. Hold a knife at an angle of 45° and draw across to make curls.

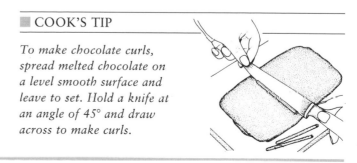

237 FRESH FRUIT SALAD

Preparation time:
20 minutes

Serves 4

Calories:
190 per portion

YOU WILL NEED:
2 dessert apples, cored and sliced
2 oranges, peeled, pith removed and
    segmented
1 banana, sliced
225 g/8 oz black grapes, seeded
100 g/4 oz strawberries, sliced
2 tablespoons clear honey
300 ml/½ pint dry cider

Mix all the fruit together in a large serving bowl. Stir the honey into the cider. Pour the liquid over the fruit and leave to cool.

Serve chilled with single or double cream.

238 NUTTY BROWN BREAD ICE CREAM

Preparation time:
10 minutes, plus
time to freeze

Serves 6

Calories:
640 per portion

YOU WILL NEED:
100 g/4 oz fresh brown breadcrumbs
100 g/4 oz demerera sugar
600 ml/1 pint double cream
100 g/4 oz walnuts, chopped

Line the grill pan with foil and brush with oil. Sprinkle over the breadcrumbs and sugar and grill until brown and crisp. Leave to cool.

Whip the cream until thick and standing in soft peaks, fold in the breadcrumbs, sugar and walnuts. Pour into a rigid plastic container and freeze until firm.

■ COOK'S TIP

*Fresh fruit salad looks
particularly splendid served
in a scooped-out
watermelon or pineapple
halves. Add the scooped-out
fruit to the salad.*

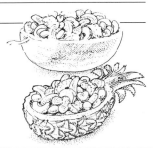

■ COOK'S TIP

*Freeze the ice cream in a
basin. When hard, dip
briefly in hot water and turn
out. Decorate with piped
whipping cream and serve
at once.*

239 PINEAPPLE ICE CREAM

Preparation time:
15 minutes, plus 4
hours to freeze

Serves 4

Calories:
275 per portion

YOU WILL NEED:
450 g/1 lb fresh or canned pineapple
50 g/2 oz caster sugar
150 ml/¼ pint water
*150 ml/¼ pint double or whipping
    cream*
2 egg whites

Blend the pineapple in a liquidizer or food processor until smooth. Dissolve the sugar in the water over a gentle heat. Add to the pineapple mixture. When cool, pour into a rigid container and freeze for 1 hour or until half frozen.

Turn out into a large mixing bowl and mash with a fork. Whip the cream until stiff and fold into the pineapple mixture. Finally whisk the egg whites until stiff but not dry and fold in. Pour the ice cream into the plastic container and freeze for 3 hours, whisking twice more during the freezing process to achieve a really smooth texture.

240 CREAMY COFFEE ICE CREAM

Preparation time:
15 minutes, plus 3-4
hours to freeze

Serves 6

Calories:
440 per portion

YOU WILL NEED:
300 ml/½ pint milk
2 tablespoons instant coffee powder
3 eggs, lightly beaten
50 g/2 oz caster sugar
1 × 410 g/14½ oz can evaporated milk
*300 ml/½ pint double or whipping
    cream, whipped*

Place the milk, coffee, eggs and sugar in a bowl over a pan of simmering water and cook, stirring continuously, until the mixture coats the back of the spoon. Pour the mixture into a large rigid plastic container, cool and freeze for 1 hour or until half frozen.

Whisk the evaporated milk until doubled in volume. In another bowl whisk the half-frozen coffee mixture until smooth. Whisk the evaporated milk into the coffee mixture. Return to the freezing container and freeze until just firm. Remove from the freezer, whisk the ice cream until smooth, whisk in the whipped cream and freeze again until firm. Accompany with cigarettes russes or other sweet biscuits and, if you like, serve with a hot chocolate sauce.

COOK'S TIP

If using fresh pineapple, cut off the leafy top and scoop out the inside. Fill the fruit shell with the ice cream, replace the lid and freeze for about 1 hour before use.

COOK'S TIP

To make a very quick hot chocolate sauce, melt Mars bars in a basin over a saucepan of hot water, or in the microwave.

Breads & Scones

Baking bread at home is not difficult and it must be one of the most rewarding pastimes. Not only is there the wonderful aroma which invades the house, but the flavour of home-baked bread is hard to beat. This chapter includes all the most popular recipes for bread, buns and scones, including muffins, teacakes and parkin.

241 WHOLEMEAL BREAD

Preparation time:
25 minutes, plus 2½ hours to rise and prove

Cooking time:
30-40 minutes

Oven temperature:
230 C, 450 F, gas 8

Makes 1 loaf

Total calories:
2325

YOU WILL NEED:
15 g/½ oz dried yeast
450 ml/¾ pint warm water
1 teaspoon caster sugar
675 g/1½ lb plain wholemeal flour
2 teaspoons salt
15 g/½ oz lard or margarine

Grease a 1 kg/2 lb loaf tin. Sprinkle the yeast over half the water, then stir in the sugar. Leave in a warm place until frothy, about 10 minutes.

Mix the flour and salt in a bowl and rub in the fat. Add the yeast liquid and remaining water and mix to a smooth dough. Turn out on to a lightly floured surface and knead until smooth and elastic, about 10 minutes. Place in an oiled bowl, cover with oiled cling film and leave to rise in a warm place until doubled in size. Turn the dough on to a lightly floured surface, knock back to release all air bubbles and knead for about 5 minutes. Shape into one large loaf. Place in the tin and cover loosely with oiled cling film. Leave to prove in a warm place until almost doubled in size, about 1 hour.

Remove the cling film and bake in a hot oven for 30-40 minutes. When cooked the load should sound hollow when rapped on the bottom. Cool on a wire rack.

■ COOK'S TIP

You may find it easier to measure dried yeast by the teaspoon. Using a proper teaspoon measure, 3 teaspoons equals 15 g/½ oz.

242 BASIC WHITE BREAD

Preparation time:
25 minutes, plus 2½ hours to rise and prove

Cooking time:
30-40 minutes

Oven temperature:
230 C, 450 F, gas 8

Makes 1 loaf

Total calories:
2615

YOU WILL NEED:
15 g/½ oz dried yeast
1 teaspoon caster sugar
300 ml/½ pint warm water
150 ml/¼ pint warm milk
675 g/1½ lb strong plain flour
2 teaspoons salt
25 g/1 oz butter
beaten egg, to glaze
kibbled wheat, to sprinkle

Grease a 1 kg/2 lb loaf tin. Place the yeast, sugar, water and milk in a jug, mixing well. Leave in a warm place until frothy, about 10 minutes.

Sift the flour and salt into a bowl. Rub in the butter. Add the yeast liquid and mix to a smooth dough. Turn out on to a lightly floured surface and knead until smooth and elastic, about 10 minutes. Place in an oiled bowl and cover with cling film. Leave to rise in a warm place until doubled in size, 1-1½ hours.

Turn the dough on to a lightly floured surface, knock back to release all air bubbles and knead again for 5 minutes. Shape the dough to fit the tin. Place in the tin, glaze the loaf with beaten egg and sprinkle with kibbled wheat. Cover with oiled cling film and leave to prove (the second rising) for about 1 hour. Remove the cling film. Bake in a hot oven for 30-40 minutes. Cool on a wire rack.

■ COOK'S TIP

Easy blend yeast is fine-textured, dried yeast which is stirred into the dry flour, then the liquid is mixed in and the bread made as for the main recipe.

243 GRAINY BREAD

Preparation time:
25 minutes, plus 2½ hours to rise and prove bread

Cooking time:
35-40 minutes

Oven temperature:
220°C, 425°F, gas 7 and
190°C, 375°F, gas 5

Makes 2 loaves

Calories:
1295 per loaf

YOU WILL NEED:
15 g/½ oz dried yeast
1 teaspoon caster sugar
450 ml/¾ pint warm water and milk mixed
275 g/10 oz plain wholewheat flour
275 g/10 oz strong plain white flour
2 teaspoons salt
15 g/½ oz butter or margarine
150 g/5 oz cracked wheat
50 g/2 oz wheatgerm
2 tablespoons malt extract

Grease two 450 g/1 lb loaf tins. Place the yeast, sugar and water and milk mixture in a jug and mix well. Leave in a warm place until frothy, about 10 minutes. Sift the flours and salt into a bowl. Rub in the fat, then add 100 g/4 oz of the cracked wheat and the wheatgerm. Mix in the yeast liquid and malt extract. Turn out on to a lightly floured surface and knead until smooth and elastic, about 10 minutes. Place in an oiled bowl, cover with cling film and leave to rise in a warm place until doubled in size, about 1-1½ hours.

Turn the dough on to a lightly floured surface, knock back and knead again for 2-3 minutes. Shape into two loaves, place in the tins. Cover and leave to rise. Sprinkle with the remaining cracked wheat and bake in a hot oven for 15 minutes. Reduce to moderately hot and bake for a further 20-25 minutes. Cool on a wire rack.

244 SODA BREAD

Preparation time:
15 minutes

Cooking time:
35 minutes

Oven temperature:
220°C, 425°F, gas 7

Makes 1 loaf

Total calories:
1805

YOU WILL NEED:
450 g/1 lb plain flour
½ teaspoon cream of tartar
1 teaspoon salt
1½ teaspoons bicarbonate of soda
350 ml/12 fl oz milk
flour, to sprinkle

Grease a baking tray. Sift the flour, cream of tartar, salt and bicarbonate of soda into a bowl. Add the milk and mix to a smooth soft dough. Knead gently on a lightly floured surface, then shape into a round. Place on the baking tray and mark the top quite deeply into four sections with a sharp knife.

Sprinkle with flour and bake in a hot oven for 35 minutes. Allow to cool on a wire rack. Break into quarters and serve sliced, with butter if liked.

◼ FREEZER TIP

Home-made bread freezes well. Put the cold fresh bread in polythene bags and suck out all the air with a pump. Seal, label and store for up to 6 months.

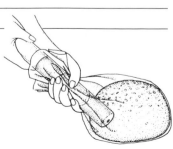

◼ COOK'S TIP

For a change, divide the dough into 8 pieces and make round rolls, cutting a cross in each. Bake at the same temperature as the loaf for about 15 minutes.

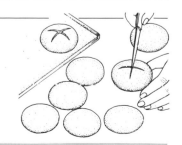

245 PITTA BREAD

Preparation time:
25 minutes, plus
2-2½ hours to rise
and prove

Cooking time:
35-40 minutes

Oven temperature:
240 C, 475 F, gas 9

Makes 8

Calories:
290 per pitta bread

YOU WILL NEED:
15 g/½ oz dried yeast
1 teaspoon caster sugar
about 450 ml/¾ pint warm water
575 g/1¼ lb strong plain white flour
½ teaspoon salt
2 tablespoons vegetable oil

Flour four baking trays. Place the yeast, sugar and half the water in a jug. Mix and leave until frothy.

Sift the flour and salt into a bowl. Add the yeast mixture, oil and enough of the remaining water to mix to a firm but pliable dough. Knead and leave to rise as Basic White Bread (recipe 242).

Turn out on to a lightly floured surface. Shape into eight equal-sized balls. Cover and leave to rest for 30 minutes. Roll out each to a 5 mm/¼ inch thick oval. Place on the baking trays, cover and leave to prove in a warm place for 30 minutes.

Cook on the lowest shelf of a very hot oven for 5 minutes. Do not open the oven until the time is up. Transfer the tray to a higher shelf and cook for a further 3-5 minutes, until the pittas are puffed and lightly browned.

Split and fill with a salad, if liked.

COOK'S TIP

Make the pitta bread using wholemeal flour. Brush the shaped loaves with a little water and sprinkle with sesame seeds before baking.

246 NAAN BREAD

Preparation time:
25 minutes, plus 1½
hours to rise

Cooking time:
15 minutes

Makes 12

Calories:
120 per naan

YOU WILL NEED:
1½ teaspoons dried yeast
150 ml/¼ pint warm milk
1½ teaspoons caster sugar
350 g/12 oz plain flour
1 teaspoon salt
½ teaspoon baking powder
150 ml/¼ pint natural yogurt
small knob of butter

Place the yeast, milk and sugar in a jug. Mix well, then leave in a warm place until frothy, about 10 minutes.

Sif the flour, salt and baking powder into a bowl. Add the yeast mixture and yogurt and mix well to make a soft dough. Turn out on to a lightly floured surface and knead until smooth and elastic, about 10 minutes. Place in an oiled bowl, cover with cling film and leave to rise in a warm place for 1½ hours.

Turn the dough on to a lightly floured surface, knock back to release all air bubbles and knead for 2-3 minutes. Divide into 12 equal pieces. Roll into balls, then flatten into large oval shapes.

Lightly butter a griddle or large, heavy-based frying pan and heat until very hot. Cook the bread ovals, one or two at a time, until the underside is golden brown and the top begins to bubble. Turn and cook the second side. Repeat with the remaining dough pieces. Serve hot or warm, with Indian or spicy dishes.

COOK'S TIP

Naan is an Indian bread traditionally baked in a tandoor – a charcoal-fired clay oven. It is served with most main dishes or dals to mop up the juices.

247 MUFFINS

Preparation time:
25 minutes, plus 2
hours to rise and
prove

Cooking time:
15-25 minutes

Makes 10

Calories:
205 per muffin

YOU WILL NEED:
15 g/½ oz dried yeast
½ teaspoon caster sugar
300 ml/½ pint warm milk
1 egg, beaten
25 g/1 oz butter, melted
450 g/1 lb strong plain white flour
1 teaspoon salt

Flour two baking trays. Whisk together the yeast, sugar and half the milk in a jug. Leave in a warm place until frothy, about 10 minutes.

Mix the egg with the remaining milk and the butter. Sift the flour and salt into a bowl. Add the yeast and egg mixtures and mix to a soft dough. Turn on to a lightly floured surface and knead until smooth and elastic, about 10 minutes. Place in an oiled bowl, cover with cling film and leave to rise in a warm place until doubled in size, about 1½ hours.

Turn out the dough on a lightly floured surface and knead for 2 minutes. Roll and stamp out 10 rounds with a 7.5 cm/3 inch plain cutter, re-rolling as necessary. Place on the floured trays, cover with cling film and leave to prove for 30 minutes.

Lightly grease a griddle or heavy frying pan. Cook the muffins a few at a time over a moderate heat for 5-8 minutes each side, until well risen. Leave to cool on a wire rack. Serve split and toasted with butter.

248 CROISSANTS

Preparation time:
1 hour, plus 2-2½
hours to rise and
time to chill

Cooking time:
10-15 minutes

Oven temperature:
220 C, 425 F, gas 7

Makes 12

Calories:
200 per croissant

YOU WILL NEED:
25 g/1 oz fresh yeast
3 tablespoons water
200 g/7 oz butter
2 teaspoons salt
1½ tablespoons sugar
150 ml/¼ pint milk
350 g/12 oz plain flour
beaten egg, to glaze

Cream the yeast with water. Put 25 g/1 oz of the butter into a bowl with the salt and sugar and pour over the milk. Cool to lukewarm, then add yeast and flour and knead until smooth. Cover and leave to rise until doubled in size. Knead the dough, wrap in an oiled polythene bag and chill thoroughly. Roll out on a floured board into a rectangle 13 × 38 cm/5 × 15 inches. Dot a third of the remaining butter over the top two-thirds of dough. Fold in three and roll out, then fold again. Chill for 30 minutes, then repeat twice more.

Roll out dough to three 30 cm/12 inch squares. Cut squares into four triangles. Roll up each and form into crescents. Put on a floured baking tray. Prove for 30 minutes. Brush with glaze and bake in a hot oven for 10-15 minutes.

■ FREEZER TIP

Pack muffins in a polythene bag when cold. Defrost in the microwave on full power, allowing about 15 seconds for 1, 30 seconds for 2 and 1 minute for 4.

■ COOK'S TIP

When rolling fat into dough do not allow the dough to become greasy. Chill it frequently between rolling, putting it in the freezer for 10 minutes.

249 TEA CAKES

Preparation time:
25 minutes, plus
1½-2 hours to rise
and prove

Cooking time:
20-22 minutes

Oven temperature:
220 C, 425 F, gas 7

Makes 8

Calories:
270 per tea cake

YOU WILL NEED:
450 g/1 lb plain flour
1 teaspoon salt
2 teaspoons sugar
100 g/4 oz currants
25 g/1 oz fresh yeast
300 ml/½ pint warm milk
melted butter, to brush

Sift together the flour and salt. Add the sugar and currants. Cream the yeast with a little extra sugar and some of the warm milk. Pour this mixture into a well in the centre of the flour, scatter flour lightly over the yeast and leave in a warm place for 10 mintues. Add the rest of the milk, mix to a light dough and knead well. Cover the bowl with cling film or a cloth, and put in a warm place to rise, until doubled in size, about 1-1½ hours.

Knead again, divide into eight, roll and shape into round tea cakes. Prick each one with a fork. Put on a warmed greased tin, cover with a cloth and stand in a warm place to prove for 30 minutes. Bake in a hot oven for 10-12 minutes, brush with melted butter and return to the oven for 10 minutes. Serve each cake split in half, lightly toasted and spread with butter.

250 HOT CROSS BUNS

Preparation time:
40 minutes, plus
1½-2 hours to rise
and prove

Cooking time:
20-25 minutes

Oven temperature:
220 C, 425 F, gas 7

Makes 12

Calories:
250 per bun

YOU WILL NEED:
450 g/1 lb strong plain flour
1 teaspoon salt
1 teaspoon ground mixed spice
½ teaspoon ground cinnamon
50 g/2 oz butter
1 sachet easy-blend dried yeast
50 g/2 oz caster sugar
100 g/4 oz currants
50 g/2 oz chopped mixed peel
150 ml/¼ pint warm milk
4 tablespoons warm water
1 egg, beaten
FOR THE GLAZE
50 g/2 oz granulated sugar
3 tablespoons milk

Sift the flour, salt and spices into a bowl. Rub in the butter. Stir in the yeast, sugar, currants and peel. Make a well in centre and add the milk, water and egg. Mix to form a soft dough. Turn out on to a lightly floured surface and knead until smooth and elastic. Place in an oiled bowl, cover with cling film and leave to rise in a warm place until doubled in size, 1-1½ hours.

Knock back the dough, then shape into 12 balls. Place well apart on greased baking trays and flatten slightly. Cover with oiled cling film and leave to prove for 30 minutes. Remove cling film, slash a cross in each bun. Bake in a hot oven for 20-25 minutes. Bring the sugar and milk to the boil, stirring. Brush over the buns. Cool on a wire rack.

■ FREEZER TIP

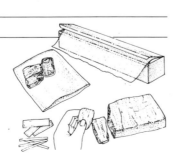

Fresh yeast can be frozen. Wrap small pieces in cling film, then pack in a polythene bag. Store for up to 6 months.

■ FREEZER TIP

Make the buns in advance and freeze them unglazed. When defrosted, put them in a hot oven for 2-3 minutes, then glaze them.

229 CHOCOLATE MINT CHEESECAKE

Preparation time:
30 minutes, plus 1½ hours to chill

Cooking time:
5-10 minutes

Serves 8

Calories:
630 per portion

YOU WILL NEED:
75 g/3 oz butter
225 g/8 oz plain chocolate digestive biscuits, crushed
FOR THE TOPPING
450 g/1 lb cream cheese
50 g/2 oz caster sugar
100 g/4 oz plain chocolate, melted
2 eggs, separated
few drops peppermint essence
3 tablespoons hot water
15 g/½ oz gelatine
150 ml/¼ pint double cream, to decorate

Lightly grease a 20 cm/8 inch loose-bottomed cake tin. Melt the butter in a saucepan, add the crushed biscuits and mix well to coat evenly. Press evenly over the base of the tin and chill until set.

In a mixing bowl beat the cream cheese with the sugar, melted chocolate, egg yolks and peppermint essence. Place the hot water in a small bowl and sprinkle over the gelatine. Stand over a saucepan of simmering water and stir until dissolved. Cool slightly and stir into the cream cheese mixture. Whisk the egg whites until standing in soft peaks and fold in. Pour over the biscuit base and chill until firm.

Remove the cheesecake from the tin. Whip the cream until stiff and pipe around the top of the cheesecake.

230 PROFITEROLES

Preparation time:
20 minutes

Cooking time:
25-30 minutes

Oven temperature:
220 C, 425 F, gas 7

Serves 4

Calories:
860 per portion

YOU WILL NEED:
150 ml/¼ pint water
50 g/2 oz butter
75 g/3 oz plain flour
pinch of salt
2 eggs, lightly beaten
FOR THE FILLING
300 ml/½ pint whipping cream
FOR THE CHOCOLATE SAUCE
100 g/4 oz plain chocolate
75 g/3 oz butter
3 tablespoons golden syrup

Put the water and butter in a saucepan and heat gently until the butter melts, then bring rapidly to the boil. Remove from the heat and quickly stir in the flour and salt until the mixture leaves the sides of the pan clean. Allow to cool slightly, then beat in the eggs a little at a time. Beat well until the paste is smooth and glossy. Spoon teaspoon-sized balls on to a greased baking tray. Bake in a hot oven for 20-25 minutes until well risen, golden and crisp. Remove from the oven and split each profiterole. Cool on a wire rack.

Whip the cream, then use to fill the profitroles. Place on a serving plate. Melt the chocolate, butter and syrup over a gentle heat. Pour over the profiteroles and serve immediately.

■ COOK'S TIP

If a loose bottomed tin is not available grease and line a 20 cm/8 inch deep cake tin and place double thickness foil strips in a cross to lift out set cheesecake.

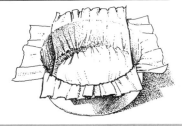

■ COOK'S TIP

Choux pastry items should be cut open immediately they are removed from the oven to allow steam to escape and prevent them becoming soft.

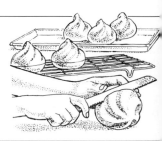